Teaching in a Cold and Windy Place: Change in an Inuit School

In 1987 Joanne Tompkins travelled to a Baffin Island community to take on the job of principal at a local school. This is the fascinating story of her experiences during the four years she spent there and the many challenges she faced.

On her arrival in the Inuit village, Tompkins found struggling teachers and failing students in a community that was grappling with social and economic change. Outlining strategies that worked and others that failed, she gives a vivid account of the day-to-day trials and rewards that she and community members experienced as they worked to create a rich and productive school environment.

This engaging and informative account will be of great use to educators and administrators and will appeal to general readers as well. One educator who read the manuscript paid it the compliment of comparing it to Sylvia Ashton-Warner's classic tale of teaching Maori children, *Teacher*.

JOANNE TOMPKINS is a lecturer in Diverse Cultures, Sociology of Education, and First Nations Education in the Department of Education at Saint Francis Xavier University.

Teaching in a Cold and Windy Place

Change in an Inuit School

JOANNE TOMPKINS

UNIVERSITY OF TORONTO PRESS
Toronto Buffalo London

© University of Toronto Press Incorporated 1998
Toronto Buffalo London
Printed in Canada

ISBN 0-8020-4168-X (cloth)
ISBN 0-8020-8030-8 (paper)

Printed on acid-free paper

Canadian Cataloguing in Publication Data

Tompkins, Joanne Elizabeth, 1961–
    Teaching in a cold and windy place : change in an Inuit school

    Includes bibliographical references and index.
    ISBN 0-8020-4168-X (bound) ISBN 0-8020-8030-8 (pbk.)

    1. Inuit – Education – Northwest Territories – Baffin Island.
    2. Educational change – Northwest Territories – Baffin Island.
    Tompkins, Joanne Elizabeth, 1961– . I. Title.

    E99.E7T66 1998   371.829'971207195   C98-930560-0

University of Toronto Press acknowledges the financial
assistance to its publishing program of the Canada Council
for the Arts and the Ontario Arts Council.

'This is a cold and windy place.
The children living here need to learn how
to live in and appreciate this place.'

– Anurapaktuq elder, 1990

Contents

Acknowledgments

Many people helped me complete this monograph. I thank the Government of the Northwest Territories, the Northwest Territories Teachers' Association, and the Baffin Divisional Board of Education for granting me leave, during which this work was completed. Lynn McAlpine, my adviser, gave me support, guidance, and feedback on an on-going basis. Claudia Mitchell and Nancy Jackson encouraged me early on that this topic was worthy of research and they continued to provide support as readers of this paper. Many professors and fellow students in the McGill Department of Curriculum and Instruction helped and challenged me to clarify my thinking.

Jacqui Bishop Kendall deserves special mention as the exemplary teacher and kindred spirit who shared so much of what happened in the work described here. I hope she can see herself written into the monograph. I thank Fiona O'Donoghue for being my mentor and guide during my time in the North. I am grateful to Father LeChat for the advice, guidance, and wisdom that he offered during our time together in the Eastern Arctic.

I would like to thank my parents and my brothers for the love and encouragement that allowed me to venture far from home. I thank my husband Ed for his love, support, enthusiasm, insight, and patience during this entire project. His work on formatting and conceptualizing this project are most appreciated. Finally, Marion and Frank deserve a big thank you. They came along part way through this adventure and were very patient with me while it unfolded.

Finally I would like to thank the people of Anurapaktuq – the children, the parents, and the teachers of that community – for their graciousness and for teaching me some important lessons about education, culture, and life in general.

Teaching in a Cold and Windy Place:
Change in an Inuit School

Prologue

School-based education, in the form of federal schools, has only formally existed in the Eastern Arctic for the past thirty-five years. There were schooling efforts by the Roman Catholic and Anglican missionaries beginning in the late 1800s (Blacklead Island). Although most schooling was largely catechetical in nature, there was a high degree of literacy achieved among the Inuit during this period (Hinds 1958). Compared to many other native communities in Canada, formal education here is still barely out of its infancy. However, in thirty-five years the pattern of evolution of formal education there has not differed greatly from that in other native communities. There is basically the same history, during the early 1960s and 1970s, of colonial supremacy and displacement of native language and culture by the school system occurring in the Eastern Arctic. The 1980s and 1990s have brought a growing awareness of the importance and indeed necessity of including native people in the design and control of their own education. The Baffin Divisional Board of Education, a totally Inuit-controlled board, was incorporated in 1985. In 1987 the board began production of Piniaqtavut, a program of study designed to reflect the linguistic and cultural needs of Baffin students. By 1989 the number of fully certified Inuit teachers (those who completed the Eastern Arctic Teacher Education Program) reached 40 out of a total teaching pool of 165, and there were at least 50 Inuit teacher-trainees in schools. Nonetheless, in 1990 many schools still failed Inuit children. The drop-out rate of children in the Eastern Arctic remains high (Diubaldo 1985).

Cummins (1986), drawing on research on minority students around the world, has concluded that minority students frequently become disabled educationally as a result of their interactions with often well-intentioned educators. At the school and the classroom level there exist many overt and covert institutional practices that lead to student failure. Cummins outlines important interventions that he feels will help schools become sites of success rather than failure.

This monograph is the story about a school that in 1987 was failing to meet student needs, and which through many interventions, some suggested by the work of Cummins, became four years later a school that was hopeful and productive and well on the way to meeting the needs of all the students in the community. It is written in the form of a detailed narrative in which I try to record and later analyse what I did as principal, and what we did as a staff, to create positive change in the school.

The role of an educator anywhere is not easy, but certainly there are tremendous challenges in teaching in the Eastern Arctic, where profound social and cultural changes have happened in a very short time. Educators often do not know how to break the cycle of despair and disappointment that greets them in the schools and communities in which they teach. Some of this story will speak to educators in minority settings and aboriginal communities and will be most applicable to native communities. Some of it concerns issues in pedagogy and good teaching practices, and will address the wider context of small schools in economically impoverished, remote settings. My prime readership is intended to be Baffin educators. I invite other readers to take what can be generalized and apply it to their context.

This story is my attempt to outline strategies that worked and were successful in one Baffin community. I hope that by detailing these strategies and the process of change that occurred, I might be able to help other principals, particularly in the Baffin, and possibly in other communities that share a similar context, be successful in their role. The average turnover rate of principals in the Northwest Territories in 1990 was 2.3 years. Fullan (1988) suggests that creating institutionalized school change is a three- to five-year process. It seems clear that many Baffin principals become overwhelmed by the nature of their assignments and leave before they are able to affect change. Principals often fall into the trap of 'blaming' – either the kids in the school, the teachers, or the parents in the community – for school failure. I hope this monograph will help principals to see the 'big picture' within which they work, while at the same time outlining in detail the kinds of strategies that I think were effective in one northern community. For the purposes of this monograph, I have changed the actual name of the community to Anurapaqtuk, meaning 'place that is usually windy.' It is really only one person's voice, recording school change and then reflecting on the experience, but I hope it will be a voice that speaks honestly and practically in an encouraging way to those educators who really want schools to be sites of success rather than failure.

CHAPTER ONE

Telling the Story

This chapter describes the methodology that I used to create this story so that the reader will have a rationale and an understanding for what is to follow in the next five chapters.

> Narrative is the study of how humans make meaning of experience by endlessly telling and retelling stories about themselves that both refigure the past and create purpose in the future.
>
> Connelly and Clandinin (1988, 24)

Psychological Context

It became clear to me very soon after I arrived in Anurapaktuq (meaning 'place that is usually windy') in 1987 that I was involved in an incredibly interesting journey, personally and professionally. Shortly after we began making initial changes, I began to see evidence of change in both student and staff behaviour. Community people began to comment on the different 'feeling' in the school. I felt that I was becoming involved in something exciting in the school and that it was necessary to record what was happening there. I felt that I needed to keep my impressions, feelings, and ideas in a journal so that I could record how the process of change occurred, and also so I could refer back to the journal as a way of showing how my thinking was evolving. I kept the journal over a four-year period and wrote in it twice a month. The journal also provided a means of reflecting on my actions and trying to interpret the context in which I was working. Sometimes, in the absence of support around me, I used the journal to express my frustrations or doubts about the job, about myself as principal. The longer I stayed in Anurapaktuq the more I was aware of the changes that were occurring and the depth to which I was being influenced and changed by the environment around me. I came to understand educational, cultural, and political issues in new ways. I came to know aspects of life, friendship, tragedy, family, and community that I had not previously known. All in all, the four years spent there affected me in a profound way and I wanted to be able to record in some way part of that experience.

As time went on, I began to realize that the changes occurring in Anurapaktuq were noteworthy. From feedback from visiting consultants to information gained from the school review conducted by the Baffin Divisional School Board in January 1989, to improvements in attendance patterns, to informal community feedback it became clear that the climate and the culture of the school were changing and that it was necessary to share these successes so that other schools could see that change was actually possible in a far from perfect world. Through sampling of written work we were able to notice improvements in both Inuktitut and English in the students. The need to share information about these changes and the change process, particularly with other school principals, became apparent. Many principals, especially those who lacked northern experience, found it very difficult to see where they could start tackling the problems of attendance, staff morale and development, and student underachievement. I felt that if such changes could take place in a community with as many challenges as Anurapak-tuq, then surely there was no reason why similar changes could not be implemented in other Baffin communities.

At the time I went to Anurapaktuq I knew very little about educational research and had little inclination to ever partake of it. I had an idea of pursuing studies at the graduate level, but that was thrown far into the future. I saw the school and the research field as totally separate entities, without any intersection. However, in my third year in Anurapaktuq I attended a conference in which the keynote speaker, Angela Ward (1990), spoke about research that took place in schools and classrooms rather than in labs and universities – a kind of research where educators could work in the field – and that was perfectly legitimate and useful research. For me it was an important turning point. I began to see that theory and practice did not have to be so separate (Schön 1983). From that point on I viewed the journal and other information I was collecting as perhaps one day leading to a 'story' that might help other educators. At the time I was also being influenced by stories from other educators, such as *McDonough 15: Becoming a School* (Carmichael 1981), about a principal who attempted to lead change in an inner-city school in Louisiana, and *Teacher* (Ashton-Warner 1963), in which Ashton-Warner talks about her journey with Maori children. I was moved and influenced by these works and excited by their 'educator-friendly' style. Later, when I applied for and was accepted into a graduate program in education, I realized I had begun to develop a framework into which I could place my own research.

Research Design

Situating this study of the change process in Anurapaqtuq within a research paradigm that would prove to be accessible and useful to fellow principals was one of my biggest concerns. Based on my own experience and discussions with other principals, I have come to believe that what happens in classroom practice is often unaffected by current research. Conversely, the 'multiple realities' (Fullan and Hargreaves 1991) that teachers live in the classroom – what really happens in classrooms – is seldom the object of research and examination. I hoped to produce research that would be useful to me and to other principals in the Baffin. In order to understand the framework that I would choose for my research I had to come to understand basic questions related to knowledge and reality. Guba (1990) provides a good summary of these issues in his discussion of paradigms. He states that before deciding on a methodology one has to look at one's assumptions about ontology and epistemology or, in other words, decide on the nature of reality, on the relationship of the inquiry to the known, and on the direction the inquiry should take. There should be congruence among the three factors. Guba describes the major knowledge paradigms of positivism, post-positivism, constructivism, and critical theory. Through my reading and study I decided to adopt a constructivist approach, which considers that realities are relativist and exist in multiple forms of mental constructions. It follows that since realities are seen through personal and social constructions, and hence value windows, many constructions of an event are possible (Guba 1990, 25). In the interpretivist/constructivist paradigm a fusion between the knower and the known and knowledge becomes a human construction, always changing and problematic (ibid., 26). It therefore follows that if realities are constructed in the mind of the individual, then the best methodology to access these realities is through the individual's own interpretation and understanding. This led me to become a 'participant observer' in this project – recording my experiences and trying to interpret and construct their meaning. However, I do understand the nature of education to be highly ideological; so although I am relying primarily on a constructivist paradigm, I do borrow elements of critical theory that attempt to locate the individual's understanding and construction into a larger societal and historical context.

Guba is not the first to advocate the use of this constructionist approach to educational research. Up until the 1960s most educational research took the form of applied science. Educational problems were framed in the positivist paradigm as questions of science that could be answered by testing, observation, and experimentation. Since it was necessary to try to control as many variables as possible in the experimentation, much research took place outside the classroom in very controlled, often decontextualized, situations. A second paradigm of research began to evolve from this positivist tradition that attempted to look at educational problems in the context in which they occurred and to understand the multiple interpretations – the many individual and societal interpretations – that were present in any educational setting. Methodologies such as ethnographic studies, case studies, and personal narratives became acceptable forms of educational research. The subjective experience of teachers/administrators became worthy of examination and an acceptable and important avenue to increasing the understanding of educational issues. Connelly and Clandinin (1988) have used teacher narratives as an important means of having teachers reflect on past experience with a view to understanding the present and guiding future actions. Elbaz (1988) found that a personal-narrative format is an effective way to capture the non-linear, holistic, patterned, and integrated nature of what the teaching act is to teachers. It also creates a powerful tool through which to discuss schools, but more particularly in this case, in transforming the racist and disabling conditions of schools. Two powerful works done in this style are those of McLaughlin and Tierney (1993) and Casey (1993).

Methodology

This monograph falls within the interpretive view of educational theory and practice, but includes a critical component. Like Carr (1986), I feel that the 'critical character of social reality is that it possesses an "intrinsic meaning structure" that is constituted and sustained throughout the routine interpretive activities of its individual members' (85). He feels that the ways schools operate is in large part a function of how they are perceived by the 'school community.' Barone (1992) feels that the public has developed a misconception about what schools and school people are like. Reforms to the education system are based on these often incorrect perceptions. Funding and research follows from the reforms, and thus may have little to do with what schools and school people are really like. Barone feels that educators must write stories to 'help the public accept our closely observed, carefully imagined, invitingly framed descriptions of people in the public school' (1992, 22). I have therefore attempted to use a constructivist approach depicting my individual understanding of the school as accurately as possible. To this end, I have tried to write the 'story' of what happened in Anurapaktuq over a four-year period. I create the story (the narrative) from my interpretation of what happened over that period. I cite the following documents as evidence to support the claim that change did occur from 1987 to 1991: (a) my own journal excerpts, (b) school records, (c) data produced outside the school by the Divisional Board of Education and the Department of Education, and (d) my reflections after leaving the community. Before going to Anurapaktuq I had read an important work, *Empowering Minority Students* (Cummins 1986), which separated out the factors that lead to student empowerment. I used Cummins's framework for understanding the total school, and the factors or strands that he identified as a means of organizing my own narrative.

This written story, the narrative, then became the object of my own further study. I spent a year at McGill University in formal courses and reading on my own, and over an eighteen-month period I was able to discuss my ideas about education in the broad sense and my experiences in Anurapaktuq with fellow students and professors. These new interpretations led to further understanding of the experience and an ability to relate my personal experience to the experience of other educators. I hope that this reflection upon experience will lead to a deeper understanding of and a change in my practice as an educator and that these insights will be helpful to other principals in aboriginal communities. In many ways, as I indicated in the beginning of this chapter, I knew very quickly after arriving in Anurapaktuq that this was going to be a deeply lived experience. But I wanted to go beyond the experience. I wanted to be able to distance myself from the experience in order to examine it and understand it in different ways. Boud (1985) states it eloquently when he says that 'simply to experience ... is not enough. Often we are so deeply involved in the experience itself that we are unable, or do not have the opportunity to step back from it and reflect upon what we are doing in a critical way' (69).

Having kept a written journal, I was able to use that as a basis for constructing my interpretive narrative. McAlpine (1991) has outlined the various ways that writing helps to distance one from experience. She talks of writing as an artefact that can be revisited many times, that saves events in time and prevents them from being lost or changed, and that can be visited by those other than the author to see what meaning they can construct from it. She advocates writing as a way of allowing teaching professionals, especially those in training, the opportunity to deepen their understanding of the profession and improve their practices. Connelly and Clandinin (1988) have argued that one's own narrative can be constructed, reconstructed, recovered, and reconstructed again so that the author can extract meaning from it at many levels and in many ways. Personal narrative is indeed a rich tool for personal and professional growth.

Development of the Monograph

The first step in creating this interpretive narrative was to construct a description of the school changes in Anurapaktuq from 1987 to 1991. It is constructed from my reflection on the experiences in Anurapaktuq as indicated in my personal journal and also from memory, as well as from other sources of data outside the school (school reviews, school records, etc.). The very process of writing the interpretive narrative caused me to clarify my thinking on the change that was occurring. Writing has provided me with a great deal of insight into myself as a person and an educator, and I hope that other educators, particularly principals, will be able to extract understandings from my narrative and from my subsequent analysis of it. The narrative appears in the main text of chapters 3, 4, 5, and 6, and serves as the raw material, the raw data, for the secondary analysis, which is elaborated in the notes at the end of each chapter.

Having completed the construction of the narrative, I then spent time reviewing literature that validated this particular methodology. In addition, I reviewed literature related to change in education, to the principalship, and to education in aboriginal settings with the view that I would reinterpret my narrative in light of this new knowledge and understanding. Several months after having written my original narrative I returned to it and was able to look at it in a more distanced, more critical manner and to analyse my construction and gain new insights from this analysis. The secondary analysis of the narrative appears as commentaries and background notes in chapters 3, 4, 5, and 6. A short chapter at the end of the monograph outlines the major understandings that I have developed as a result of going through the process of writing this monograph.

I think it is fitting that in choosing a method of research for studying an Inuit school I chose a story format. Among the Inuit, as is the case with many native peoples, stories become important vehicles for deepening one's understanding of the simple and complex things in life. Children at the school would sit attentively for long periods of time as elders wove stories of the land, the sea, the spirits, and the people. Rudy Wiebe (1970) describes stories as being like nets that we cast out into the world; if well-crafted they allow us to capture the gems of life – the deeper understandings, the important nuggets of truth. As a Qallunaaq* and one who speaks very limited Inuktitut, I cannot hope to understand 'story' in the sense that Inuit understand it. However, the more I began to read stories or the more I watched students and fellow teachers relate to Inuit stories, the more I came to understand their elusive power. A story that appeared to have no relationship to me and my life would later come back to me at a time when I needed it. Having the privilege of working with Inuit has helped teach me the value of stories and, very appropriately for this research, the important value in visiting the same stories over and over again to gain new understanding.

---

* Qallunaaq is the term Inuit use to describe non-Inuit people. It is the term generally used to describe southerners, like myself, who came to the North. It is a descriptor and does not generally have any perjorative sense.

CHAPTER TWO

The Context of Anurapaktuq

This narrative is written about a part of Canada that is far away in distance and sometimes in time from mainstream Canadian life. It is important for the reader to understand the context in which this story takes place; hence, I have included this chapter as a means of trying to situate the reader in my shoes. I describe the history, ecology, and sociology of the community itself and I also try to describe my own history, which greatly influences the ways in which I was and was not able to interact with the community. For purposes of this monograph I have changed the name of the community and the names of teachers in the school.

Historical and Ecological Context

The Baffin region of the Canadian Eastern Arctic covers an enormous land mass and extends from a southerly latitude of 56° 32′ North at Sanikiluaq in Hudson Bay to its most northerly latitude of 76° 25′ North at Grise Fiord, high up on Ellesmere Island. Baffin Island is the world's fifth largest island. The administrative region of the Baffin includes the twelve communities on Baffin Island itself, the communities of Igloolik and Hall Beach located to the west of Baffin Island on the Melville Peninsula, the community of Sanikiluaq in the Belcher Islands in Hudson Bay and the northerly communities of Resolute Bay and Grise Fiord located on Ellesmere Island.

Anurapaktuq, a village of five hundred people is located in the Baffin region on the shores of a large and shallow basin of the Arctic Ocean. This basin provides a rich habitat for walrus, whales, and other sea mammals because of the plentiful, year-round supply of molluscs upon which walrus and bearded seals feed. The abundance of these marine

The Inuit have lived in the Baffin region for over 3500 years, since they emigrated east across the land bridge from Russia (McGhee 1981). As early as 2000 BC, Pre-Dorset people were living in small groups along the coast of this area, where wildlife was plentiful (Crowe 1969). These people were replaced later by the Dorset culture, which appears to have developed from earlier palaeo-Eskimo culture. The technology of the Dorset that has remained, which includes many articles developed for hunting on snow and ice, indicates that the climate at the time of their existence may have been colder than that of the Pre-Dorset people. The Dorset culture lasted until around AD 1300 and was replaced by the direct ancestors of present-day Inuit, the Thule people. The Thule borrowed some technology from the Dorset group, mainly the snow house and the snow knife, but went on to develop a rich technology that included the kayak, the umiak (large skin boat), the bow-drill (for fire production), and the bird dart. The ruins of several Thule houses can be found within a short walk from the present settlement of Anurapaktuq. The modification from the Thule tradition to the present-day Central Eskimo tradition seems to have been made around the seventeenth century, when a cooling climatic period appears to have forced many of the whales to leave the area.

For the next two hundred years the Central Eskimo people flourished in small camps around this area. They had inherited and developed a complex technology that allowed them to exploit the rich resources of the sea around them and also to make use of the resources on land.

Up until the early 1800s the Inuit mainly lived in very small extended-family groups throughout the Baffin region, mostly along the coast of the island where there was a constant food source. There was limited contact between the small nomadic groups. Relative to other native groups in Canada, contact with Europeans came much later for the Inuit of the Eastern Arctic. During the late 1600s and the 1700s there was some contact between European explorers, such as Frobisher and Franklin, and Inuit, but these were usually quite isolated, limited to small groups of Inuit, and brief in nature. In the 1800s whaling activity brought many American and Scottish whalers to the Baffin area and the two cultures influenced one another. Inuit hunters and guides often provided the whalers with valuable expertise in hunting and survival skills for the Canadian north. Many a ship had to winter over in the Baffin, and the Europeans often survived thanks to the help of the Inuit guides and families in the area. Whaling activity was particularly vigorous in the area around Anurapaktuq, where sea mammals were plentiful. The whalers were able to offer employment, trade, and novelty, and even changed the settlement patterns of the Inuit, bringing them together in larger groups that eventually turned into settlements. From the Europeans the Inuit obtained many items that they quickly incorporated into their material culture: rifles, cloth, tea, tobacco, flour, and steel knives were readily adopted for Inuit use. Unfortunately, the Inuit were often exposed to many European diseases to which they had little or no resistance and often the results were tragic. Items such as alcohol and tobacco also created illness related to lifestyle. The whaling period prospered and lasted until the early 1920s and was considered a 'boom time' in the Eastern Arctic. However, in the 1920s the market demand for whale products declined rapidly and whaling activity ceased quickly in the North.

The period from 1920 to 1945 can be characterized as one of general neglect by most of the world, especially the Canadian government, towards the Inuit. There were some traders, mostly working for the Hudson's Bay Company, who established posts to trade white fox furs with the Inuit. These traders preferred the Inuit to continue their land-based existence and did not wish to have Inuit living permanently near the trading posts. Missionary activity began in an active way during this period, with the Anglican and Catholic missionaries working among the Inuit. The work often focused on bringing the 'Good News' to the Inuit and converting them to Christianity, but missionaries also often served as paramedics, trying to fight epidemics and lessen some of the worst features of the whaling industry. To this day, most Inuit in the Eastern Arctic remain devout Christians. One major activity of the missionaries that affected a great many Inuit near Anurapaktuq in the 1950s was the establishment of a church and residential school at Chesterfield Inlet. The residential-school experience for the Inuit, like most First Nations people, often resulted in familial and cultural alienation. In recent years, allegations of sexual and physical abuse have been levelled against several residential school staff members at Chesterfield Inlet.

Generally, the number of missionaries throughout the Baffin was small and the area to which they ministered was huge. The RCMP also established a presence in the North during this time, but again their presence was limited to a few settlements. There were some anthropologists and scientists conducting research on the Canadian north during this period (Thule Expedition, Soper) and the Canadian government did send a patrol boat with some medical care around to the various posts. But for the most part the number of Europeans permanently living on Baffin Island during this period numbered no more than a few dozen in a vast and expansive land.

The period after the Second World War marked the beginning of a high level of government activity in the Canadian Arctic and the beginning of a period of rapid cultural change for the Inuit. The Canadian and American governments began constructing the Distant Early Warning System (DEW line) across the northern frontier to act as a defence system in case of attack by the Russians. There was a great deal of construction work that brought hordes of southerners to work in remote parts of the Baffin. Where there had previously been no year-round, permanent settlements in places like Anurapaktuq, communities started to grow and Inuit moved to these communities to seek employment. At the same time, stories of the neglect of the Canadian government towards the Inuit were starting to reach the general public in southern Canada. A change in the migration patterns of the caribou and a reduction in some herds led to starvation for some groups of Inuit. Images of Canada's starving Inuit prompted the public to demand that health, education, and social services be provided for Inuit just as they were for every other Canadian citizen. This period also coincided with the optimism of the Diefenbaker years and the dream that Canada's future lay in the untapped oil and minerals riches of the North. There was a feeling that with modern, improved technology, people, including southerners, would be able to conquer the North and set up comfortable living there. Thus, in a brief twenty-year period, from 1950 to 1970, most Inuit went from living in small, seasonal camps around Baffin Island to residing in permanent, year-round settlements where services such as nursing stations, schools, Hudson's Bay stores, airports, and missions were located. Housing sprang up and a range of related municipal services grew to meet the needs of the population (Crowe 1969). Infant mortality declined as a result of access to medical care and the birth rate grew in the Eastern Arctic to its level today, where it is four times the rate of that in southern Canada.

Sociological Context

A DEW line site was built near what is today Anurapaktuq in the early 1950s. Soon several Inuit families began to gravitate towards this site in search of employment. As these families began to settle near the base, the government, which was in a period of expansion in the North, began to establish services in the community of Anurapaktuq, located approximately 3 kilometres from the radar site. Crowe (1969) gives a detailed description of the growth of the village during this period. A nursing station was built in Anurapaktuq in 1957. A two-room school and Hudson's Bay

Company store were constructed in 1967. By 1968 there were 260 Inuit living in Anurapaktuq and there were 60 buildings extending along the beach, including an Arctic Co-operative and a Roman Catholic mission. A sea-docking area and impressive air hanger compound were built near Anurapaktuq to service the DEW line, and these facilities afforded the village with more access to the South than neighbouring communities of similar size would have had.

As happened in virtually all the Baffin, great cultural change has taken place since the 1960s as Inuit have tried to adjust to a life away from the land. Anurapaktuq was no exception. A good description of the social organization of the community in the late 1960s is found in Crowe's work (1969). He describes the fourteen social organizations in the community, ranging from the Housing Association, the Inuit Council, and the RCMP to the missions and the commerce and youth organizations. Of these fourteen organizations, all were from outside the Inuit tradition and only the Anglican mission and the co-operatives showed signs of increasing participation by Inuit. Crowe describes the Inuit society of Anurapaktuq at that time as still being largely 'land-based,' although people had moved in from the camps and were living in permanent dwellings. He felt that the society still maintained a camp structure, with a man's status being measured by his hunting ability and with the elders playing an important role in maintaining traditional law and values within the community. Most elders had either direct or indirect links to community organizations, so although they did not necessarily exercise direct control over community decisions, their influence was still present, though often subtle. It appears that as Anurapaktuq was becoming established as a settlement, there were two systems operating. One was a more mainstream model, which held most of the power in the community; the other was a more traditional model, which held limited power to influence the direction of change and growth in the community.

In the late 1960s it became apparent that grave problems were facing Inuit as they moved into settlements such as Anurapaktuq. By 1968 the regional job structure had absorbed as many of the adult, unschooled Inuit as it wished. Part of the government rhetoric in the construction of the DEW line was that the project would provide employment for local people. In 1968, with 100 per cent of the local population being Inuit, 80 per cent of all jobs went to workers brought in from southern Canada. Of the 690 Inuit living in both Anurapaktuq and a neighbouring community, only 33 were employed by the DEW line in 1968 (Crowe 1969). Crowe looked into the future and foresaw that northern development did not have the interests of the Inuit at heart. Decisions made in Ottawa and Washington were profoundly affecting the lives of Inuit. Crowe worried that unless Inuit were able somehow to enter into the discussion, decisions about their future would be made for them, not by them.

In the late 1980s when I arrived in Anurapaktuq, the people were still struggling with the challenges of acculturation that Crowe described. The DEW line never did mange to employ more than a small handful of local Inuit on a full-time basis. The few positions that Inuit held were usually at the lowest level and often took men away from their families for several months at a time, which created strain on the family unit. As well, the DEW line had negative effects on the hamlet by making alcohol available to the community. DEW line employees, most often single men, fraternized with women, especially younger women from the village, and often permanently disrupted family units in Anurapaktuq. Many men fathered children there, yet never stayed long enough to provide support for those children.

Inuit did not manage to enter into the workforce at any senior level in the community. Most of the top jobs in the service field (teachers, RCMP, nurses, store managers) were held by Qallunaaq. Some Inuit were employed by the local hamlet to drive trucks or work at the clerical level, but for the most part there were high rates of unemployment. Sea mammals and caribou were plentiful in the area and people still were active in hunting. The use of dogs has continued in Anurapaktuq until the present day, even though it has ceased in many other communities. The government continued to build up the service sector into the 1980s; however, it could not keep up with the growing birth rates and migration of people off the land. Housing supply could not keep up with demand, and there are severe conditions of overcrowding in the community.

Anurapaktuq is similar to other Baffin communities in its broad history; that is, in the development from nomadic existence to contact with Europeans, to semi-nomadic existence, to, finally, establishment of a settlement. However, from the point of view of the empowerment of local people, Anurapaktuq did not develop as well as some communities. The effect of the close proximity of the DEW line to the settlement had many negative effects, as previously stated. From an economic point of view the community is also disadvantaged. The flat, windswept landscape does not call out to tourists in the strong way that the mountains and glaciers of other Baffin communities do, and therefore tourism has not developed as it has in other hamlets. While most other Baffin communities were able to create some employment related to tourism, Anurapaktuq could not. The problem became cyclical. As there was no tourist infrastructure offering adequate hospitality facilities in Anurapaktuq, opportunities that would have spurred the local economy, such as regional and territorial conferences and meetings, special visits by dignitaries, and tour packages, passed the community by. To make matters worse, money that might have come from the Arctic arts and craft movement through the sale of carvings and prints did not come to Anurapaktuq. The local soapstone, which is dull grey in colour and of poor quality, did not compete well in the southern market. Local ivory is plentiful and is used for carving, but because it has been poorly marketed, local artists have not enjoyed the same success in ivory sales as other communities. The lack of employment in the community outside of the handful of jobs on the DEW line (which came at a high social cost) has had a discouraging effect on the community and has forced many members to live in conditions that come with unemployment. Poverty, overcrowded housing, drug and alcohol abuse, and domestic violence are social problems that grew out of this economic despair. Trying to deal with these huge and complex issues has drained energy and hope out of many of the residents, energy and hope that otherwise could have gone into community development.

Another example of the underdevelopment of the community is the lack of community facilities. Anurapaktuq has been one of the last Baffin communities to request and receive facilities such as a community hall, a skating rink, and a modern school – facilities that are standard in most other communities. It is one of the few communities without a coffee shop – a common gathering place for young people. The effect of poor facilities cannot be overestimated in small, remote places. Community members would travel to other communities and see more modern facilities, then begin to assume that other places were better than Anurapaktuq because they had such nice facilities. Schoolchildren particularly noticed how inadequate their facilities were when they travelled to schools that had such things as gyms and libraries. Government people travelling to the community would note the poor condition of the hotel, the school, and the community hall and assume, incorrectly, that the local people did not care about their community. The arguments became cyclical and self-fulfilling. These are but a few indicators of the low esteem in which the community was viewed by its own members and by outside people.

Anurapaktuq – Present Day

As I outlined above, the Anurapaktuq that I arrived at in 1987 was not one of the more advantaged of the Inuit communities in the Baffin region. The community did not have the spectacular vistas and mountains of certain other, more photographed, communities. The day I first flew into the community it was a grey and overcast. A fog hung over the basin. Small ice pans dotted the water and the big ice lay not far offshore. There was little vegetation on the gravel moraines and raised beaches that spread out as far as the eye could see. Greenish brown ponds dotted the flat gravel landscape and were filled with waterfowl getting ready to make their August departure. The day was cold, rainy, and windy, and unlike other Arctic communities where the moisture brings out sand and mud, the limestone in Anurapaktuq turned into a whitish clay that splattered everywhere. Unfortunately, Anurapaktuq is not one of those communities that displays itself well on such a grey day. One has the sense of a desolate, poor, forlorn place set in the middle of nowhere.

Given a sunny, blue-sky day the whole perspective of the landscape changes. The waters off the shore are brilliant blue and dotted with vibrant white ice pans. Often marine mammals can be seen from shore and the waters are active with hunters. One can walk for miles on the clean gravel and marvel at the tiny but courageous Arctic plants that cling bravely to the rocks, or search for fossils along the moraines. The ponds are filled with bird life and to be out on the ponds on a clear day watching the families of loons as they feed is to experience wilderness in its truest sense.

However, I was only to discover the natural beauty of Anurapaktuq at a later date. Its physical beauty was hidden from me on that first day. The grey and dismal feeling of the place was not enhanced by much that I saw as I drove through the village. There was and continues to be a severe housing shortage in the community. Though several new, modern, freshly painted 'Greenlandic' houses (in the style of Greenland homes – that is, two-storey dwellings with fairly pointed roofs) had been constructed along the beach front, many of the houses were crowded and looked in need of renovations or at least a good painting. Several qarmaqs (large canvas tents with wooden doors) were set up along the beach, either as summer dwellings for people or for families who could not afford or maintain public housing.

The public buildings in Anurapaktuq in August 1987 included

– The Anglican church with its battered grey-asphalt siding in an imitation brick design with yellow trim that is common to most Anglican buildings in the Eastern Arctic;
– a Roman Catholic mission painted yellow on top and green on bottom;
– a small Hudson's Bay store recognizable by its white paint and red trim;

- a larger green Eskimo Co-op store, which looked as if it had been made by piecing several shacks together;
- a brand new two-storey health clinic that towered above everything else in the village;
- a small two-room government office (originally a two-room housing unit) that had served as the original school in the community;
- a renovated bungalow on the beach that housed the Hamlet Office and the local radio station;
- a small RCMP office and jail cell located at the far end of town on the way to the dump;
- several grey garages that housed such thing as the firetruck, the water truck, and the sewage truck for the hamlet;
- a low building made of several obsolete two-room housing units pieced together, badly in need of paint, covered with graffiti, and with a leaky roof, that served as the community hall – the only recreation facility for the community and by far the worst facility of its kind in all of Baffin; and
- several other low-lying buildings that served as garages and warehouses for various agencies such as the Housing Association and the Department of Public Works – all again badly in need of repair and a good painting.

But in all of this, quite likely the most desperate and sadly neglected of all the buildings seemed, at least to me, to be the school.

The School

The school stood right in the middle of town, on the main road next to the Hudson's Bay store. It was of a design common to many Arctic community schools built in the late 1960s: a long rectangular building with four classrooms down one side, a hallway in the middle, and offices, washrooms, a teachers' room, and kitchen down the other side. Behind were two portable classrooms. Owing perhaps to a surplus of brown paint in the government warehouse, many of these schools were painted in a dark chocolate brown. Not exactly something that helped to accentuate vitality and creativity. The paint on the school was peeling and several boards had been ripped off the building, probably by bored students. Some of the windows had been broken over the summer and been boarded up with plywood. The doors were beaten up and sadly in need of paint. Some of the letters in the school name were falling off. Overall, the effect was quite dismal, and at least outwardly this building seemed tired and abused.

Later I grew not to notice the outside appearance of the building because the inside was so unfavourable for learning. Often the sewage system backed up, leaving the smell of sewage hanging in the halls. The building had little or no insulation, meaning harsh hot days in August and May and mostly cold, uncomfortable days during the rest of the year, when the open waters off Anurapaktuq combined with the relentless winds to make the village the 'coldest spot' in the Baffin for weeks at a time. There was a chronic lack of space to house people or things. Classrooms were overloaded with children, and there was no place to put supplies. The staff room, kitchen, and main office were converted into work and teaching areas. No one room had the luxury of having only one function – everything, including the hallways and the bathrooms, served dual purposes. When I arrived in 1987, the capital plans called for the construction of a new school in the 1989/90 school year. Consequently, it was felt that it was not worthwhile to put money into a building that would be demolished in the near future. As it turned out, construction delays meant the new school did not open until January 1991, three and a half years after my arrival in Anurapaktuq.

Ironically, however, being in such an awful physical plant helped me to realize that good programming is not strictly dependent on good facilities. Lack of space and lack of facilities are often used as excuses not to carry out innovative programs. Some of our most successful programming took place in spaces the size of the cupboards in that old school – the 'kids in kupboards' program, we liked to call it.

What was of greater concern to me as principal and program support teacher entering Anurapaktuq was the state of the school program. In the eight years before I came to Anurapaktuq (1979–1987) there had been four changes of principal in the community. The mainstay of the teaching force at that time were Qallunaaq teachers from southern Canada. There was only one certified Inuit teacher in the school. There had been high staff turnover among the Qallunaaq educators, fairly typical of that time, with the average Qallunaaq teacher staying only two years in the community. Such a high rate of turnover at the classroom and school level had a serious effect on in-school programs and had strained community relations with the school.

The effect on school programs was a lack of clear vision for the school. Although direction did come from the regional office of the Department of Education during this time, before the development of the Baffin

Divisional Board of Education and its mission statement 'Our Future is Now' (BDBE 1988), the direction of each school developed almost autonomously at the community level. The development of the school from year to year was uneven and dependent on the particular leadership in the school at the time, and within the school the quality of programs varied greatly from class to class. The role of the principal at that time was ill defined, and most principals were themselves full- or part-time teachers with little chance to help and support other staff even if they so chose. There were exceptional teachers who taught in Anurapaktuq and who did wonderful things with children. Often, however, there was no system in place for those teachers to share their skills and talents with less experienced members on staff.

The difficulties of this community/school relationship were described to me by a man who had been a principal in Anurapaktuq for seven years (in the early 1970s, before the period of rapid principal turnover) during a meeting I had with him before going to the community. I hoped to try to gain as much understanding about the community dynamics as I could before going there, and I felt this principal's impressions gleaned over several years might help me to understand the community's development. This principal felt that for several years in the 1970s the community had had fairly stable staff and the relationship between the school and the community had been generally positive. As the school grew larger and as staff turnover increased, he felt, the community began to believe that the Qallunaaq staff did not like the community or the children because they left the community after one or two years. Community members became less comfortable being in the school environment. The new Qallunaaq teachers who arrived in the community sensed the community's standoffishness and interpreted it to mean that the community did not care about the education of the children. At this point there were few if any Inuit educators in the school to help Qallunaaq teachers with their perceptions of the community. Consequently, these teachers became frustrated with what they perceived to be the lack of community support and did not stay long. In a sense, both the Qallunaaq teachers' and the community's perceptions were true, and a vicious cycle began. The Community Education Council was in its infancy during the 1970s and 1980s and, as a result, direct input by the community in the school was minimal.

The program in the school before my arrival in August 1987 looked like this. There was a combination of teachers and classroom assistants, who later came to be called 'teacher-trainees,' working in the school.

Teacher-trainees were local people hired to work in the school and act as a partner with a certified teacher, complementing the language and culture component in the classroom program. Teacher trainees could take twelve-day intensive courses throughout the school year and at summer school, and after ten courses were eligible to take a final year at the Eastern Arctic Teacher Education Program and receive teacher certification through McGill University. During the 1980s many teacher trainees ended up playing a very secondary role in the classroom; many were 'stuck' in their role as a helper, rather than a partner, and were not working towards certification. In the mid to late 1980s their title was changed officially from 'classroom assistant' to 'teacher-trainee' to remind the trainees themselves, other teachers, and the school administrators that local people should be working towards achieving full teacher certification and thus becoming increasingly present in the northern teaching force.

In Anurapaktuq kindergarten was taught by a teacher-trainee, who received very little support and guidance in planning a kindergarten program. The program only took place in the afternoon and attendance was usually high. Instruction took place in Inuktitut, but written material in Inuktitut was almost non-existent. Several children had been held back in kindergarten and the school's policy on promotion was unclear. Because the kindergarten class was held in the library, it was difficult to set up a permanent classroom arrangement there. Grade 1 was conducted by an Inuit teacher, who taught a large class out in a portable classroom. Though a more experienced teacher, she was working in physical isolation from the rest of the school. Materials in Inuktitut were lacking, but instruction was in Inuktitut. Grades 2/3 and 4/5 were taught by Qallunaaq teachers, who had the support for part of the day of Inuit teacher-trainees. The children received some instruction in Inuktitut, but most of the instruction took place in English. The Grade 5/6 class was taught by the principal. On paper, the principal was supposed to have administrative time to attend to principalling, but in reality there were no substitute teachers in the community and the teaching job was a full-time assignment. Furthermore, there was little time available for the principal to do administrative or leadership tasks. The Grade 7, 8, and 9 students were taught by a Qallunaaq teacher in another portable.

Program delivery and instruction varied greatly from one class to another in the school. In some classes children were working in math textbooks and workbooks; in others a hands-on approach was used. Some classes were very traditional, with rows set up and most instruction done in a large group using a 'transmission' method. In others there was more use of small groups and centres. Some classes were taught reading using a phonics approach in both languages; others were trying out more holistic methods.

The amount of Inuktitut taught in the school varied depending on the grade. After Grade 1 the amount of time the children spent learning in Inuktitut diminished greatly. The two senior classes (Grades 5/6 and 7/8/9) received forty minutes a day of Inuktitut instruction from an Inuit elder hired by the Community Education Council. Unfortunately, little support was available for this unilingual Inuktitut speaker; she was left on her own to 'teach Inuktitut,' although materials were lacking and she had never had any teacher training courses or workshops. The reaction of the older children towards Inuktitut instruction was predictably not very positive, and they often considered it a free period. The children in the community came to school speaking Inuktitut, which was and still is widely used in the community and in the homes. The children's written and reading skills in Inuktitut, however, were generally very weak, and this did not contribute to their sense of pride in their culture or language.

The materials and supplies in the school reflected the various pedagogical trends in the school over the last dozen years. Scores of textbooks and reading series lay gathering dust on the shelves as teaching methods changed or as people found them inappropriate. Housing the supplies was difficult as space was at a premium; materials were stored in every available, and unfilled nook and cranny. To my delight two wonderful teachers from the previous year had spent the 1986/87 school year organizing materials in the library so that resource material could be located by teachers. Baffin schools usually do not have librarians, and material retrieval is often an impossible task. The other important procedure that these two talented teachers, Dawn and Bill Loney, initiated was to create theme boxes in the school where material on relevant teaching themes could be stored and later referred to. As a result, when we embarked on theme teaching later on we had some idea of how its organization might take place. Generally, in 1987 we were left with good supplies by the previous staff for setting up classroom programs. Money had been redirected from the purchase of textbooks into more resource and hands-on material and lots of book-making materials, chart paper, and art supplies that would serve us well as we tried to develop a more active approach to learning through the school.

Attendance in the school was among the lowest in Baffin (67 per cent in 1985), with morning attendance being a problem. Because of unclear policies on student promotion over the years, the age distribution in each class varied greatly and some students who had spent several years at the same level and had lost a lot of interest in learning. At the intermediate and junior-high level students who did not succeed in school generally dropped out of the program. Without a gymnasium children had little opportunity for a proper physical-education program and the school lacked a central meeting place where school-wide events could be held.

Having travelled across the Baffin myself for two years as a Program Support staff member, I was able to gain certain general impressions of communities and of children from a bird's-eye view. I can recall that my impressions of the children in Anurapaktuq – and this is confirmed by other consultants travelling through the region – were generally of outgoing, friendly children. They did not seem to go through the 'shy' stage that is common among children one meets in the North, but rather would come up to a person on the street and start conversation.

The situation in Anurapaktuq and throughout the Eastern Arctic has many facets and it is difficult to assess the amount of 'progress' that has been made in the last twenty-five years. Depending on where one looks, it is possible to see hope as Inuit take steps to establish their own territory of Nunavut where they will have self-determination; or it is possible to see despair as one looks at the lifestyle illnesses that affect many Inuit in the form of suicide, chemical dependency, and spousal and child abuse in a context where unemployment is high and there appears to be only an increasingly bleak economic future ahead. Irwin paints a most disturbing scenario for the Inuit when he says:

The reality emergent in the Arctic is a reality in which a growing Inuit population will come to live in larger, and possibly more regionalized, communities and towns. If current trends continue, rates of unemployment will not improve, even though the number of job opportunities may rise. Although Inuit families will decline in size, they will probably be more numerous, requiring expanded housing and social services. Should migration remain a socially undesirable and economically high-risk strategy for members of this poorly educated population, then most of the Inuit can be expected to remain in the Arctic, even though they will probably have lost more of their language, culture, and land-based skills. If this description is correct, then most of the Inuit living in the Arctic in the year 2025 will probably be second-generation wards of the state, living out their lives in 'arctic ghettos' plagued by increasing rates of crime. (1989, 2)

It is against this mixed backdrop of hope and despair that I arrived in Anurapaktuq on that August day in 1987.

Psychological Context

Teaching anywhere is no small task, but teaching in Nunavut presents certain unique challenges. Formal education is relatively new to the North and to communities like Anurapaktuq. The first school was built in Anurapaktuq in 1967, so in 1987 the community had only had direct experience with formal education for less than twenty years. During that period there were great changes in how education was viewed. In the early 1960s instruction was almost completely in English, by Qallunaaq teachers from southern Canada. There was no curriculum in place in the early days, so curriculum was borrowed from other provinces and was gradually replaced by a Northwest Territories curriculum which remained very southern based. Qallunaaq teachers were often well meaning, but usually the content and language, and even teaching strategies, were so foreign to the students that many did not do well in school. Teacher turnover was high, which disrupted programming for students. Attendance was often poor and parents generally did not understand or have much input into the aims of education. Two good books that give a more complete account of the challenges, joys, and frustrations of teaching in the 'earlier days' in the North are written by Hinds (1958) and Macpherson (1991).

It became apparent in the 1970s that Inuit children were not doing well in the formal education system. Most students who began school in kindergarten dropped out before they finished junior high school. Colbourne states that 'the outcomes of schooling in terms of extremely high dropout rate (10 times the national average) and cultural erosion constituted a remarkable phenomenon in a system designed to prepare individuals for a modern northern lifestyle' (1987, 14).

Attempts were made in the 1970s to include native speakers of the language in the classrooms to help facilitate learning, and there was some recognition that Inuit culture should be present in the school, but usually these two measures were add-ons to a program that was still foreign to the students. The Territorial government's *Survey of Education* (1972) represented the government's first steps to examine the effectiveness of its schools. In 1981/82 a 'Special Committee on Education' was set up to travel across the NWT and talk to communities about education. The committee's report, *Learning, Tradition and Change* (GNWT 1982), set up the framework for the changes that would take place in education in the North and in the Baffin. Its major recommendations were that the first language and culture of the children be seen as strengths upon which to build a foundation of learning, that programs for all children should be community based, that all special-needs students be educated with age-appropriate peers in their community schools, that the training of native teachers become a priority, that parents play a more active role in schools, and that divisional boards of education be set up in each of the major regions of the NWT.

I arrived in the Baffin in 1982 on the heels of the *Learning, Tradition and Change* document, when I accepted a job as a primary teacher in the village of Pangnirtung in the Baffin region. Teaching proved to be a challenge. Pangnirtung was typical of most Nunavut communities. Children were supposed to be taught in Inuktitut from kindergarten to Grade 3. In cases where there were no Inuit teachers for these classes, southern teachers worked with an Inuk teacher trainee. The intent was that the teacher would provide the pedagogical support for the trainee, who would bring the linguistic and cultural component into the school. Such was my case in teaching Grade 2/3 for three years in Pangnirtung. Grades 4 and 5 were considered transition years between English and Inuktitut; sometimes there was a classroom assistant to help out at this level, and sometimes students went into a totally English classroom unsupported. From Grade 6 to Grade 10 the courses were taught by Qallunaaq teachers, with the children going out for brief periods of Inuktitut language and cultural activities.

What was asked of a teacher at that time, and what is asked now, is quite demanding. Good teachers everywhere should have a strong understanding of how to individualize instruction for the wide range of students in a class. The wide ability level found in any regular southern class is perhaps further widened in the North by factors of second-language usage and varying attendance patterns on the part of the children. With the inclusion of special-needs students into regular classrooms, the need to individualize is even more apparent. Teachers must have a good understanding of first- and second-language learning and be able to accommodate students in an English as a Second Language (ESL) situation. Qallunaaq teachers should be able to work effectively in a cross-cultural situation – with children, with fellow workers, and with the larger community. All teachers, Inuit and Qallunaaq alike, must also have good skills in programming in order to create relevant teaching plans, often in the absence of useful materials or guides. And it would help immensely if teachers had some first-hand understanding of poverty and isolation so they could start to understand some of the forces at work in the community. Ambitious challenges indeed!

When I arrived in Pangnirtung in 1982 I knew little about the job that I was supposed to do. I had spent my early years growing up on Cape

Breton Island, Nova Scotia, so I had some sense of what isolation might be like. I came from a family tradition that was closely linked to the Antigonish movement of the 1930s – a self-help movement that tried to help the 'little people,' the farmers and fisherman, gain more control over their lives. From that tradition and from listening to stories told over the supper table I learned about the ability of people to change the conditions of their lives through working together. I had a great belief in the ability of people, given the right conditions and support, to change and become 'masters of their destiny.' This conviction was important in helping me believe that things in Anurapaktuq could change. From my high school and university days, when I worked and studied in the field of recreation, I had acquired a good deal of experience working with people, and especially with children. To this day I feel that the skills I learned in trying to teach children in swimming pools, canoes, drop-in centres, summer camps, and around campfires helped me as much in the classroom as any formal teacher training I received.

Not that my teacher training was bad – in fact, it was probably a little better than in most other universities, in that we spent more time in classrooms. I did my education degree at a French university, so I learned something about language teaching and something about being in a cross-cultural situation. I did not learn very much about how to 'teach.' Most of the theory we learned was largely divorced from the act of teaching and the 'practice' teaching sessions did not allow much time for real 'practice.' Most student teachers were expected to carry out the work of the classroom teacher in the absence of any feedback, support, or modelling from good teachers. Once you had your certificate you became a 'trained' teacher, so everyone expected you to be trained. Therefore, once you had your own class you were not supposed to need help, even though you'd never had a real period of 'training.' And thus a cycle of unprepared teachers begins. So I graduated in 1982 with my teaching certificate in hand, an interest in teaching, virtually no knowledge of native peoples, a lot of previous experience with children, some ideas about second-language teaching theory as it related to French and English, but precious little understanding or skill in how to put together a program of study for children, particularly Inuit children.

I had two reasons for wanting to go north to teach. The first was that I wanted to teach in a small community where I would have a real opportunity to come to know the parents of the children whom I would teach. I had spent time living in rural parts of Nova Scotia and knew that I could, although I enjoyed what cities offered, be quite happy living in a small community. The community where I completed my teacher training had a population of 350 people, and I delighted in the richness it had to offer. I also had a notion that I wanted to go to the North. I had seen most of Canada from coast to coast, but knew that I probably wouldn't get to see the third coast unless I went there to live. A cousin of mine who had gone to Spence Bay on the Arctic Coast years before had enjoyed the experience. I did have a sense at the time that I could be an enthusiastic and, I hoped, good teacher and that I could offer a lot to the children with whom I would work. I had a lot of energy and no family responsibilities, and knew that I would become actively involved in community life. I had a sense that teaching was an important career and a good way to serve one's fellow human beings. I think it was a sense of venturing into the unknown and a feeling that I would learn a lot from living this far out of the mainstream that prompted me to accept my first teaching assignment in Pangnirtung in 1982.

The first thing that I had to do after I hung up the phone from accepting my job in Pangnirtung was to get a map and find out exactly where Baffin Island was and then where Pangnirtung was! I knew little of the geography of the North and almost nothing about the Inuit with whom I would be working. I did have some notion of the plight of Canada's native peoples from a Canadian Studies seminar that I took in high school, but I quickly realized it was a very minimal understanding.

Pangnirtung was a lucky first placement for me in many ways. First, I landed in the 'Switzerland of the Arctic.' Pangnirtung is a beautiful settlement situated on Cumberland Sound on the east coast of Baffin Island and is surrounded by incredible mountains. It is rich in history and was an active whaling site in the 1800s. One of the older settlements on Baffin Island, it has a well-developed community infrastructure. The climate is warmer than settlements to the north and the mountains block the cold winds that blow further north.

From a teaching point of view I benefited greatly from working for three years in the primary area of the school, where in the company of many skilled Inuit and some Qallunaaq teachers, I was able to learn a great deal about the teaching process. There is nothing like teaching young children to really teach you about teaching. I worked with a trainee who taught me as much about the Inuit culture and working with Inuit children as I ever taught her about teaching. In this class I was fortunate to have the opportunity to hear Inuktitut on a constant basis, and so was able to gain a limited proficiency in understanding the language.

While in Pangnirtung I was also able to work under the direction of an influential northern educator, Charles (Chuck) Tolley, the principal at Pangnirtung, who later became director of the Divisional Board of Education. Chuck is a seasoned Northerner who had spent seven years in the community and over twenty years in the Arctic. Chuck taught me a great deal about history and vision and about the relationship between the two. He has a great sense of the history of the North and particularly of the Cumberland Sound area, and is able to help bring that alive for people. He also has a historical perspective on the development of education in the North. When people would be about to give up in despair and say things would never get better, or when people (especially new southerners) would offer 'solutions' to northern education ten minutes after getting off the plane, Chuck would be able to help give them a perspective on where things were coming from. Chuck also holds an immense belief in Inuit people to make intelligent decisions about what they wanted for their children's future. He feels that for years stupid decisions about native people had been made out of Ottawa and Yellowknife (the territorial capital). He trusts far more the ability of someone from Pangnirtung to make an intelligent decision about their son or daughter on location! And, importantly, perhaps because of his sense of history, he understands that things would not happen overnight and that patience, vision, and faith are required.

I left Pangnirtung after three years to accept a job as a Program Support staff member in the board office in Iqaluit, the Baffin region administrative centre. In 1985, as a result of *Learning, Tradition and Change*, the Baffin Divisional Board of Education had adopted a policy that students with special needs would be provided with community-based education mainstreamed into regular classes with their same-age peers. Previously, many students with special needs either were in institutions in southern Canada, were not coming to school, or were sitting in classes without any kind of program supporting them. My job was to be part of a team of three who would travel across the Baffin region and help teachers integrate these children into their programs. Although I did not have formal training in special education I had learned a great deal about individualizing instruction, particularly though the use of activity centres in my classroom, and had started to work with other teachers on this task. In many ways, my lack of formal training in the 'specialization' model allowed me to approach the challenges of mainstreaming from a fresh, perhaps naive, but functional perspective. The job challenged my beliefs about education and forced me to consider the important philosophical questions of who we teach, what we teach, and how we teach.

In my two years travelling through the Baffin I was deeply influenced by four people. Two of them – Fiona O'Donoghue and Linda Makeechak – were exceptional women who helped me deepen my own views about education. From Fiona I learned that every child had the right to be, and could be, educated with same-age peers. She debunked the myths that have built up around special education and helped me learn that good education means that all children can be included in the program. Like Chuck, she has an intense belief in the ability of Inuit parents and teachers to make wise and intelligent decisions about the education and care of their children. She was a pioneer in the Baffin who sought out children who had never been students because no services were available to them and their families previously.

Like Fiona, Linda had worked with students with special needs and believed that they had much to learn, as well as to offer, in the regular classroom program. Linda is a woman of incredible physical and moral strength. She fervently believes that all students with special needs, at whatever level of functioning, could be integrated into regular classrooms. In the beginning, before the days of ramps and accessible buildings, she would be dragging wheelchairs up stairs into buildings and through town to prove that the only real barriers to integration were those in people's minds. Both these women are incredibly hard-working, determined individuals, and if it meant moving mountains to get children into classrooms, these two would be ready to start lifting the rocks!

A third person who influenced me greatly is my husband Ed Miller. I first met Ed when he came up from the Montreal Children's Hospital to help us with behaviour management in classrooms. As children with emotional and behavioural difficulties were being integrated into regular classrooms, we needed training in behaviour management from someone who believed that the regular classroom was the place where all children should be educated. In my experience children with behaviour problems were the most challenging students to integrate into regular classroom programs. Ed introduced the phrase 'Catch 'Em Being Good,' which encapsulated his views on behaviour management. He feels that if we could spend more time catching others doing the good things they are doing and less time noticing when they screw up, people would be more inclined to keep doing good things. Ed feels that teachers missed numerous opportunities to notice kids doing good things and, likewise, that principals miss numerous opportunities to reinforce teachers who were working hard and trying to do the right thing. Ed also taught me to be patient. Through example and words he taught me that people change in small steps – not all at once – and that we have to be there to reinforce each small step as it happens. Ed taught me that you can aim high and expect people to reach those heights as long as they are reinforced for trying and not punished for failing. A major part of our school philosophy in Anurapaktuq became based on 'Catching 'Em Being Good.'

The last person who greatly influenced my formation before I moved to Anurapaktuq was Geela. When I met Geela she was fifteen years old and living in the community. She was a girl who was very big, hemiplegic, and mildly mentally handicapped. Before 1982 she had attended the community school, but unfortunately had not moved along with her peers. When she was first assessed in 1983, she spent most of her time in a primary class, where she was supposed to be the 'helper'; but she was more considered part of the class, was teased by the children, and had developed some inappropriate behaviours. From 1983 to 1985 Geela had the support of a Special Needs Assistant, and a program that focused on life skills was developed for Geela to supplement her school program. By 1985 Geela was turning sixteen and would have been of age to attend high school in Iqaluit. For various reasons – academic, social, and family – it was felt that Geela would benefit from the experience of high school. It is important for the reader to get an idea of who Geela was before she left the community. She was big and quite awkward and was often teased by children. She spent half her time chasing younger children through the village. Being almost incapable of acting appropriately with peers or other adults, Geela quickly resorted to a teasing/chasing relationship with these people. She had learned some life skills, but generally was not independent in this area, and her appearance was unkempt and messy. She spoke Inuktitut and some English and had a remarkable ability to repeat entire phrases that she heard. Having to sustain a conversation of more than a few words, however, was difficult for Geela. She had few activities besides watching TV, with which she could entertain herself independently.

At that point in the development of a mainstreaming model at the Baffin board, Linda and I were at a loss how to integrate Geela into a high school program that was largely academic and involved many different teachers because of the high school rotary system. We proceeded with Geela's placement using trial and error since we did not have many models to follow anywhere in Canada. At that time challenging needs children were just beginning to be integrated in elementary schools; high schools were still too rigid to allow mainstreaming. The first trap we fell into was using the developmental model for programming. This model assumes that all children regardless of their age and ability pass through the same developmental phases in the same order. In the case of Geela, we would find out what tasks she could do now, and then look at a developmental chart to see what would be the next tasks for her to learn. This model does not look at the context in which a student lives to determine what skills need to learned. Nonetheless, we assessed Geela using this model and figured that, since she had not developed number concepts, we should start programming for her in that area. Fortunately, with the help of some strong feedback from Geela, we quickly realized that she was only going to have two to three years left in school and there were many more important things than counting that she had to learn – like how to have friends and how to express her needs appropriately. Gradually we came to realize that what Geela most needed to learn could be learned by being with people her own age and by being expected to act like a teenager. For Geela that meant starting with things like look-ing to see if someone's coming through the door before barrelling through it. It meant not playing chase in the hallway or screaming 'Fuck off' at the top of her lungs every time something didn't go her way. It meant learning the names of some girls in her class and how to stand around at recess and have a conversation with other people. Geela spent some time in classes, with work geared to her level, and sometimes she worked on her own, learning how to access the community around her and how to develop interests and hobbies that could make her life more interesting.

One of my only regrets in working with Geela is that we did not take weekly video footage of the changes that Geela went through. I can tell you of the changes because I witnessed them and I know where Geela started, but if the reader could observe Geela from where she started to where she is now, one would have to believe in the power of change. Six months after her arrival in Iqaluit Geela was barely recognizable from her Anurapaktuq days. Her own aunt, on a visit to Iqaluit, did not recognize her in church. In the first six months she had lost weight, learned to carry herself as a teenager, learned how to groom herself, and donned teenager's clothes. But more important were the changes in Geela's person. She could initiate conversation, she could be appropriate with peers, and she even started to have friends in school. To me it was a powerful demonstration of how, if you organize the environment in such a way as to encourage growth and development, people will respond. My family tradition had instilled in me an intellectual sense that change was possible, but with Geela I witnessed that change in a real and emotional way. Working with Geela also reinforced in me the importance of having a vision, and a belief in that vision and having the patience to work towards that vision one step at a time. There were certainly lots of reasons never to have let Geela leave her village. After all, this kind of thing had never been done (how often are things left undone because 'that's never been done'), what if we failed, what if Geela hurt someone ... a lot of 'what if's'! However, a combination of our ignorance, our idealism, and bloody hard work by Geela and by a whole group of people around Geela – from teachers to students – made this remarkable transformation take place.

I also took another mentor with me through the writings of Jim Cummins, who had come to Baffin to speak at a teachers' conference about ways to empower minority students. I had a copy of his most recent work at the time, *Empowering Minority Students*, which outlined practices that would lead schools to become places where students would become more empowered. Cummins's studies of student success in North America and Europe found that in situations where a child is of a minority culture and that culture is not the dominant culture students achieve better in school when they are taught in their first language for at least the first three years of their school career (Cummins 1986). Inuit students would be considered to be in a minority position vis-à-vis the dominant Canadian society, even though they make up the majority of students in Nunavut. Cummins advocated first-language instruction first to enhance both cognitive development and self-esteem. Cummins's framework became an important model for me in Anurapaktuq.

I learned a lot of important things about education, people, and change while doing the job of Program Support person, one of the most important being the role of programming in education. A well-planned program was the key to classroom success for students. However, in far too many cases, as Linda and I would try to plan a math program for a student with special needs we would become acutely aware that the math program for the rest of class was poorly planned and, in some cases, totally lacking. The beauty of the model of special education implemented in the Baffin was that it allowed us to help teachers with the whole issue of program planning through the guise of special education. Program Support Teachers (PSTs) were hired as in-school consultants to help teachers individualize instruction for the children with special needs in their classes. By improving the program offered to all students in the class, the teacher would be able to accommodate students with special needs. We were really talking about programs meeting the needs of every kid – not just those with special needs.

I had learned since my arrival just how challenging the work for teachers is in the Baffin. Working in a bilingual, bicultural setting with many levels in the class is a considerable challenge. In my work in the classroom and with teachers I became convinced of the need for real support mechanisms at the school level to help teachers put good programs into place. Left on their own, without intervention, little islands of good teaching will emerge in classrooms where experienced teachers have figured out how the pieces go together. In the less fortunate classrooms, struggling and often inexperienced teachers will simply try to get by, and little real learning takes place.

My two years as a Program Support staff person were exhilarating, exciting, rewarding, frustrating, and most of all exhausting. Most of our time was spent in airplanes and living out of suitcases, working in communities. I loved the opportunity to see so many communities, to have the privilege of working with so many teachers, to be in so many classrooms, to see Baffin schools from a board-wide perspective. I was able to observe principals in different schools, and to see how they approached schooling and whether interventions they used were effective or not. But after two years I was ready to return to a more routine existence back in a quiet community. In 1987 I accepted a job as a principal and program-support teacher in Anurapaktuq. For me this move was supposed to be that return to a 'quieter life.'

CHAPTER THREE

On Change and Changes

Having set the context for the narrative in the last chapter I will now begin to tell the story. It is constructed around major themes taken from Cummins's (1986) framework. In this chapter I will provide evidence of the changes that did occur in the school from 1987 to 1991. The notes that follow this chapter represent my analysis of my understanding of the change process in light of the literature reviewed.

Evidence of School Change

Change did occur over the period from 1987 to 1991. Comparing that four-year period to the previous eight years in Anurapaktuq, or to the same four-year period in other Baffin schools, there is compelling evidence of change. To the people who have been involved in the school program and who know the children involved, there is no doubt that more children are attending school in Anurapaktuq and that they are doing better in school, both academically and socially. There are other documented measures provided by the Department of Education and the Baffin Divisional Board of Education and by community members that support this view. Essentially the major school changes that occurred during this period are improved attendance, more sense of commitment on the part of the students, increased cognitive and language development, particularly in Inuktitut, and an increase in the number of Inuit educators in the school.

In 1984/85 Anurapaktuq had one of the lowest attendance rates in the Baffin – 61.43 per cent of children were attending school (Department of Education, Baffin Region 1985). This represented one of the lowest rates of attendance in the Territories, and indeed one of the lowest in the nation. At this period many other Nunavut communities were achieving 80 per cent attendance and better. In 1987/88 the attendance had risen to 76.4 per cent; in 1990/91 the attendance was 78 per cent, with some months showing over 85 per cent attendance. This is an important increase, especially when one realizes that until recently education was not compulsory in the NWT; in some communities, like Anurapaktuq, school attendance is still not compulsory. It is safe to say that most of those children attending school are doing so because they want to be there. The review team that conducted an official school review in 1989 stated in their report: 'It was noted during the review that there is concern from staff about the number of students who come to school without breakfast, and the impact this has on their capacity to learn. This is a reality for the community, and current employment situations, as well as social conventions may mean that students will continue having to get up alone, and come to school unfed, or poorly fed. It is a positive statement on the school that attendance is as high as it is, and that an average of 80% of the students find the school environment rewarding, exciting and challenging enough to gladly attend' (Levy 1990).

As well as children coming to school more often, students are staying in school longer in Anurapaktuq. More students enrolled in junior high in 1991 than in 1985 (O'Donoghue 1991).

In addition to the amount of time students spent in school the staff tried to record improvements in the quality of students' work. Beginning in 1987 the staff worked hard to build up the students' files to include work samples of their reading and writing for each year. Improvements were being noted by teachers and were continually shared with students informally as well as twice a year in formal student/teacher interviews.

It was apparent to visitors to the school over the four-year period that the children there were generally happy and on-task. It is difficult for those in the field to actually point to measures that indicate this was so. However, as the reputation of the school in Anurapaktuq grew so did the number of visitors to the school. J. Ireland, a Baffin Divisional Board of Education consultant, had travelled to Anurapaktuq during the early and mid-1980s and not again until 1990. In personal interviews she indicated that the behaviour and attitude of the children was markedly improved in 1990. In her formal report to the Baffin Division Board of Education she stated: 'Not once in three days did I see any squabbling, jealousies, rivalries, or other negative or disruptive behaviours ... [T]hese children appear to be well on their way to developing mature emotional responses to different situations. Tension and conflict appear to have no place in this caring and helpful environment'(Ireland 1990, 6).

The School Review Team reported similar findings in its report: 'There is a tone of mutual respect in this school that is both positive and motivating. Staff greet and treat students with the utmost respect and courtesy, and this behaviour is reciprocated. As visitors to the school, you are constantly addressed by students who are confident, self-assured and positive' (Levy 1990, 5).

The school experienced change in other dimensions. One of the most significant changes, and one that had a great effect on programming, was the dramatic increase in the number of Inuit educators in the school and in the amount of time the children spent learning in Inuktitut. In 1987 a little over a third of the staff was Inuit (38 per cent) and there was only one fully certified Inuit teacher on staff. In 1991 the situation had more than reversed, with Inuit staff, virtually all of them from Anurapaktuq, making up 72 per cent of the staff. Of the fourteen members on staff only four were Qallunaaq. Three of the Inuit staff members were fully certified teachers; the rest were actively working through their teacher training program. Anurapaktuq was the first school in Nunavut, and quite probably in the NWT, to achieve such a high percentage of native staff. In 1991 a 'Principal in Training' position was allocated to the school; an Inuk teacher was trained to assume the job of principal in 1991/92. The position of assistant principal is also held by an Inuk.

Having more Inuit educators in classrooms has had a positive effect on school programs and school culture. Visiting consultants have noted that increased instruction in Inuktitut has lead to improved competence and confidence in English. Ireland, in a report on the school (1990), compared the writing of one student, Jaali, who had completed almost all of his primary education with Inuit educators in Inuktitut with another student, Lydia, who had been in classes with Qallunaaq teachers since Grade 2. She reports: '[W]hile Jaali had taken a dramatic leap in his expressive ability in a very short time, Lydia has made no such progress in a much longer time. We can only conclude that Jaali's growth has been enabled by ... instruction via the mother tongue, at a crucial stage in his intellectual development' (Ireland 1990, 9).[1]

Whereas some Baffin schools, because of a lack of Inuit staff, are still struggling to provide instruction in Inuktitut up to Grade 3, Inuktitut was the language of instruction for all children from kindergarten to Grade 4 in Anurapaktuq. Students in the junior high are receiving more instruction in their mother tongue than before, and more than in almost any other Baffin school. Statistics provided to the Department of Education indicate that, in Grades 7, 8, and 9, students in Anurapaktuq are receiving at least 40 per cent of their instruction in Inuktitut (GNWT

1991). Inuktitut is being used to teach subjects such as health, social studies, expressive arts, and language arts. The minister of education visited Anurapaktuq in May 1991 to open the new school and was so impressed by the use of first language and Inuit culture in the school that he commissioned a film to be made of the school to share its success with other communities in the NWT. The film, entitled *Together We Can Make a Difference*, was released in late 1992.

Parents have been pleased with the direction in the school. The amount of formal and informal home/school interchanges increased during this four-year period. All teachers conducted at least two home visits a year and parents were invited into the school for three formal reporting periods. The inclusion into the school program of more land activities, such as an annual spring camp, and the use of more elders as part of the program has allowed staff to interact on a more informal basis with parents. The School Review Team interviewed ten parents at random and found them to be supportive of and pleased with the school program:

> Of the parents interviewed (ten representatives), all spoke Inuktitut as a first language, and eight spoke Inuktitut as their only language. The parents were encouraged to see their children taught in a language they could understand, and felt that English should be taught later in school. All parents did state that it was important for their children to speak and read and write English and hoped that education would allow their children the opportunity of better employment later in life. The parents interviewed stated that education should allow their children greater opportunities for a variety of jobs requiring higher skills.
>
> Parents also stated that the school was a very welcoming and comfortable facility, and there were a number of 'uninvited' parents in the school during the review week affirming these characteristics. Considering the poor state of the building facility, and the lack of space, this is a very commendable achievement for the entire staff. (Levy 1990, 4)

The school has also received recognition from outside the Baffin region. The first- and third- place winners in the Inuit Circumpolar Writing Contest in 1989 were from the school. Students also placed first in the National Addictions Awareness Campaign to promote healthy living in 1989. The school won $2500 from the Reader's Digest Foundation for essays the students wrote about drugs and alcohol in 1990.

Some of the most important evidence of change comes from those who have been involved in education in the long term in Anurapaktuq.

Ooleepeeka is a village elder who has been working in the school for over twelve years. For many of those years she was an unsupported, untrained elder trying to teach Inuktitut to upper-elementary and junior-high students, often in the absence of a program and materials. She is now a teacher-trainee working with a cooperating Inuit teacher in a 'family grouped' K–4 classroom. (Family grouping is a classroom set up with mixed ages in order to promote greater individualization and more social interaction – see chapter 4.). Ooleepeeka, as a parent, grandparent, and educator, has witnessed the changes that have taken place in the school. At a workshop in 1989, when asked about what was happening in Anurapaktuq and what she thought about it, she stated: 'There are more children coming to school now and they are a lot happier when they are there' (Irqittuq 1989).

I hope that it is evident to the reader that changes did take place from 1987 to 1991 at the school in Anurapaktuq. However, as a principal I am more interested in describing how some of the above changes occurred so that other educators might realize what is possible in communities and in schools.

Process of Change

In 1987 I accepted the position of principal/program-support teacher in Anurapaktuq. (A program-support teacher is an in-school consultant who helps to provide support for programs for children with special needs.) Given the challenges to be faced in both the school and the community, I had to have a profound belief in the possibility of creating change, of making a difference in that school – otherwise I would have been crazy to accept such a position. What attracted me to Anurapaktuq was in fact the challenge in the school and the community and the belief that things could be changed, at least in the school. What was necessary throughout my four years in that community was a strong belief in creating the right conditions for people, both students and staff, to grow, and a vision of what the school could be. Not only was a belief in the possibility of people changing necessary, but I had to understand the nature of change. In 1987/88 I had completed the Principal Training Certification program for the NWT and I had learned something about the nature of educational change. One small monograph entitled *What's Worth Fighting For in the Principalship* (Fullan 1988) became an important guide for me. I learned that in order for educational change to occur you must know something both about the educational innovation itself (the content) and about how change occurs (the process). Too often in education, innovations are imposed on teachers without any understanding of how people change. I learned that, to be effective, educational change had to be a collaborative process with staff and that it would take at least three to five years to institutionalize change in school settings.[2]

In terms of working towards change in the school, my first job was to try to help build a shared vision for the school. As principal I had to try to lead people to a vision built on good educational foundations. It is difficult, especially in retrospect, to know when I was leading and when in fact I was hurrying to catch the people I was leading. Part of my difficulty in constructing this narrative is that I am not sure when to use the pronoun 'I' and when to use 'we.' I know that I had some definite ideas in 1987 about what made for good schools, and I know that I made a difference at the school. But, very shortly after my arrival at Anurapaktuq, a kind of synergism began to happen and the 'I' disappeared more and more into the 'we.' I certainly could help set up favourable conditions in the school, but it was the teachers, on the front line, who were helping kids learn and feel good about themselves. If you notice in this story that I use 'we' often it really is because 'we' achieved a rare level of teamwork in our school. In terms of building a vision we began our first week of school in 1987 by developing a mission statement.[3] I led the staff through an exercise where we talked about what kind of school we hoped to create. Then we took our rather lofty, vague statements such as 'a happy place to be' and we operationalized them so that we had measures of things we could do to show we were reaching those goals. For each of our four major goals – improved literacy, improved self-esteem, improved attendance, and improved community/school relationships – we had ten to twelve measures that would help us to keep on track. It took many other things to develop the vision once we had stated it (in-service, staff development, teamwork, and so on), but a very important part of the process was articulating this clear mission statement, first as a staff and then with support from the Community Education Council (CEC). (See appendix 1.)

One of the important factors that led to change was the increasing number of Inuit educators who joined the staff each year. 'Fortunately' we had a government housing shortage in the community and the teaching positions could not be filled by 'qualified' Qallunaaq teachers. (This is but one example of how much non-educational issues like housing can affect educational issues in Nunavut.) We had to do some creative staffing. Where other communities chose to hire Qallunaaq teaching couples or have Qallunaaq teachers live together, after discussion with my supervisor I chose to hire untrained local people to increase the number of Inuit educators in the school. It meant that we had to provide training and support on site in each classroom, but this change also quickly established a strong cultural and linguistic presence in the school, and this had great impact on the program and the morale in the school. Needless to say, it is next to impossible to create an Inuit school when most of the staff are not Inuit.

After helping to create a vision about what the school could be, the next two important things for me to know about change were that I needed faith and patience. I had to have faith that most people, most of the time, want to do the right thing. Sometimes they fail to do so because the environment is not structured in such a way as to allow them to act the way they would wish (as was Geela's case in Anurapaktuq) or sometimes they simply don't know what it is they should be doing 'instead of' what they are currently doing. I also had to learn to believe that most of the time our institutions and daily lives are set up to notice people who are screwing up and making mistakes, and we often overlook the many good things most people are doing, most of the time. As a principal I had to learn to believe that most of the students in the school were doing, and were capable of doing, good things. I also had to believe that the staff were doing the same and that a large part of my job was to create conditions that would allow people the opportunity to grow and develop ways of recognizing and acknowledging the good stuff that was happening.[4] It was a case of whether I would see the glass as half-full or half-empty, the school as half-failing or half-achieving. Would I see Anurapaktuq only in terms of the problems and the things not happening in the community and the school, or would I be able, while not denying there were real problems in the community, to focus on all the positive things that were happening in the school?

Over my four years in Anurapaktuq I learned to focus on change and on noticing and acknowledging it. I had to learn to have faith and patience that the vision would be achieved. A couple of wise friends advised me as principal to think of the staff with whom I worked as my classroom and to apply the same techniques that I would employ as a teacher with the adults with whom I worked. The relationship between us was not meant to be the often unequal relationship that exists in traditional classrooms, but more of the equal, shared relationship that we hope to create in more student-centred classrooms where teachers act to facilitate learning.[5] This powerful metaphor allowed me to see the teachers as being in the process of 'self-actualizing' or 'growing' as professionals. I was able to see that just as a teacher can create a classroom environment in which children will do poorly or well, a principal has a great deal of power to create a school environment in which teachers will want to do poorly or well. I learned that in order for teachers to grow as professionals in the new directions we would set they would have to feel secure in taking risks and acknowledged in their efforts. Using this classroom metaphor meant that I had to take risks and have courage to show my human face to the staff just as I was asking them to do in their classrooms.[6] If they feared that they would be punished or evaluated harshly for trying new strategies and ways of teaching, they would simply refuse to move. If their efforts and hard work went unnoticed or unacknowledged, they would lose interest and feel neglected. If they did not feel that their contributions mattered, they would not be team players, but would go back to closing their doors and continue to see teaching as an isolating activity. If I expected them to change all at once and did not recognize that change for adults is the same as for children – it happens one step at a time – then they would become frustrated and withdrawn.

In essence I had to model with the staff the way I hoped they would interact with each child in their class. I hoped that they would recognize that each child was at a different level and was only capable of moving forward from that location. You couldn't ask a child to be at some other level than he was, and this was true with staff. This outlook had implications for the manner in which I viewed the teaching profession. I believe that all people involved in education – from students to superintendents – are in the process of growing or are 'in-training.' And if people are 'in-training,' then they need to have on-going support in order to learn and try out new skills. Having travelled across the Baffin, I had the opportunity to be in the classrooms of many different teachers and principals, and I saw that the vast majority of them had never received training they felt was adequate to gain the skills of individualizing learning for students. Most felt uncomfortable using techniques to teach to multi-levels and many felt uncomfortable in the whole area of classroom management. All too often, poorly trained teachers are put in challenging situations where they are expected to be fully trained, are offered no real support by administrators in order to obtain those missing skills, and are then evaluated harshly when they lack those skills in the classroom.[7]

In order to have the kind of team support that was built up in Anurapaktuq, the principal must hold the view that all staff and students are moving forward – perhaps at different rates, but moving forward. The principal also has to see herself as a learner, as self-actualizing and not fearing punishment for taking risks. It was a continual struggle for me to accept my stumbling, my failures, and my mistakes and not fear punishment from myself or from others. Ultimately the way we treat others becomes a reflection of how we feel about ourselves. I believe that if the principal can provide a model of self-acceptance and acceptance of others, particularly with staff, then staff will in turn enact this model with students.[8]

What all this meant in practical terms is that a lot of time had to be spent noticing the efforts of staff and students. Even little steps must be noticed – I couldn't wait until someone had changed completely before I noticed them.[9] I had to do it every step of the way. This was another insight that I learned regarding change. It is gradual and happens one step at a time. Too often we measure change from perfection backwards and we constantly put ourselves down. Like the anorexic who is never content with the weight he/she has lost, but rather feels that she/he is always falling short of her/his goal of perfection, so too are we inclined in education to notice when the i's aren't dotted and the t's not crossed in a major essay that a student gives us.

What we had to set up in Anurapaktuq were methods of noticing the steps towards the goal. Under each of the school goals that we set, the staff and I listed a number of measures that would help demonstrate that we were making process (appendix 1). From charting improvement in student attendance and in writing over time, to increasing the status of Inuktitut in the school, I tried to develop concrete measures with the staff that would prove to our students, the community, and importantly to ourselves that we really were moving forward.

Over the course of four years the school put into practice this philosophy of 'Catching 'Em Being Good' and eventually formalized it in what we came to call a 'Discipline Policy' (see appendix 2). What it claimed to be was a preventative approach to discipline in the school, but really it was a statement about how we valued people in the school, what relationships between people should be like, and what we would do as a staff to show that appreciation. It talked about doing things like celebrating successes through assemblies, special treats, and so forth, to acknowledging staff and students each week with 'Thank You' notes, to the kinds of things we wanted to see happening in each classroom.[10] It was probably the most essential policy we had in the school because it kept everyone in the school focused on what was essential and it made us notice those things. If one looks at what people notice in a school, and if one believes that the things noticed are what's important, then one should get an idea of what is valued in a school. In some schools so much time in spent on detentions or on elaborate policies regarding what will happen if people wear hats in school that an alien visiting from another planet would think that somehow these things are what school is about. In Anurapaktuq we tried to value learning, helping, trying, working, writing, reading, math, being friends, and caring about others.

Notes

1   Cummins (1986) has stated that during first-language instruction children are not just developing skills in their first language. They are also developing a 'deeper conceptual and linguistic proficiency that is strongly related to the development of literacy in L2 [the second language]' (21). McAlpine and Crago (1992) also state that while changes in schools are often of the first order – a change in administration or curriculum – it is the second-order changes – in student-teacher behaviour and relationships – that ultimately lead to improvement in student performance. The increase of native educators not only leads to more instruction in the students' first language, but also helps to allow students and teacher to share a culture – to share thoughts and thought patterns – and to allow for the potential integration of Inuit culture in the classroom. It also provides 'for expectations of behaviour and values to be largely consistent with other aspects of life' (Flinn 1992, 7).

2   Fullan's recent work (1991) looks at educational change and gives an excellent review of the literature and the research. One major point he raises is that it is at the individual level that changes must occur. In schools that means the level of the classroom teacher. It is therefore essential for the principal to understand what is happening at the classroom level. A principal who does not see the job as involving time with teachers in classrooms is, in my mind, unlikely to influence change in the school.

3   Fullan (1991) talks about vision-building being a two-way street where principals learn as much as they contribute to others. I'm not sure if I understood this reciprocity in 1987 – I may have been like a teacher who believed it was only the children who were going to learn! Over my four years in the community and since being away I have come to see that time spent examining beliefs and developing vision are extremely worthwhile and an important foundation to the school. What I did in developing a

mission statement with staff in 1987 in a one-day workshop I would now hope to spread over several meetings and involve community members more actively. From vision should come supported action, but vision is essential. I have also learned that each year, with all staff, new and experienced, it is necessary to revisit the vision and see how each staff member has deepened his or her understanding of its meaning. At the same time that vision is being developed, I think it is necessary to participate in activities that develop trust and cohesiveness within the staff. A more cohesive staff is more likely to agree on a shared vision.

4 Rozenholtz (1989) eloquently sums up the negative cycle that happens in schools: 'Most teachers and principals become so professionally estranged in their workplace that they neglect each other. They do not often compliment, support and acknowledge each other's positive effort' (37).

5 Much of the recent literature on principalling and educational change reinforces the crucial and often overlooked role that teachers have in effecting change. Little (1981) links school improvement to teachers 'talking about their practice and building up shared language as teachers and administrators observe each other teaching, planning, designing, researching, evaluating and preparing teaching materials together.'

6 The literature on change highlights the fact that ambiguity and risk are real and necessary for change to occur, and that both teachers and administrators pass through 'zones of uncertainty' (Fullan 1991, 31). What was needed in Anurapaktuq to support these 'zones' was a sense that people could admit fear and failure. A 'culture of collaboration'(Fullan and Hargreaves 1991, 48) had to be created in which teachers and I could talk about the change process and support each other. Little (1990) has identified four main collegial relations among teachers, which go from being superficial and distant at one end of the spectrum to being collaborative and doing joint work at the other end. She feels that it is through joint work, be it team teaching, planning, or research, that collaborative cultures are built. As we shall examine in chapter 4, theme planning became one of the school's first avenues leading to a collaborative culture.

7 There is research to support the fact that teacher training does not really prepare teachers to deal with the multiple challenges of the classroom (e.g., Lortie 1975, Fullan 1991). This lack no doubt accounts for the fact that 30 per cent of new teachers leave teaching in their first year (Fullan 1991, 303). Poorly prepared teachers arrive in schools that promote and reinforce an individualistic approach, so that teachers seldom have the opportunity to watch each other teach. What is necessary in schools is an opportunity for inexperienced teachers to emulate good teachers and a system of on-going

in-service that reflects the fact that all educators in the school are 'in-training.'

Knowing the 'entry level' for the staff became an important point for me. Fullan and Hargreaves (1991) say that 'we treat teachers as if they were a homogeneous lot. In the process, we often devalue large segments of the teaching population' (28). Fullan (1991) sums it up nicely when he says that 'a real challenge for the principal is to find something to value in all the school's teachers. Good elementary teachers do this with their students and principals should do likewise with their teachers. To value the teacher one must know the teacher in order to find things to value' (87). What I had to do was to really know the people with whom I worked and try to value their difference. I couldn't really know them as long as I stayed in my office.

8 Of course, part of what I had to do was to be comfortable with my own sense of being 'in-training.' One of the truths I have learned from being in lots of classrooms is that teachers who try to over control the class (too many rules, too much rigidity, too much standardization) often end up losing control. And teachers who are more able to share power and confidence with children end up having 'more control.' As Fullan and Hargreaves (1991) advise: 'Listen to your inner voice. If the heart is preoccupied with tight control, no amount of headwork, or learned behaviour and techniques will counteract it' (89). In that sense I was on that same journey of self-reflection that the staff were on.

9 Fullan (1991) talks about the fact that, especially in the early stages of implementing change, it is important to notice and reinforce changes in behaviour.

10 Fullan and Hargreaves (1991) stress the need for celebrating steps towards change on the part of students and teachers. 'Celebrate staff and students' contributions to achievement, in public presentation and staff meetings; writing private notes to express thanks for special efforts; encouraging and supporting teachers to share experiences with each other; participating in informal celebrations; revealing something of one's private self as a person; asking for help where appropriate; and show that one is vulnerable, not invincible' (89). This whole attitude of caring had to pervade all interactions in the school, and I hoped that my attempt to model caring, noticing, and giving encouragement in my relationships with teachers would lead them to model the same behaviour with their students.

CHAPTER FOUR

The Program

In this chapter I discuss the strategies that occurred at the classroom and school level that I feel led to change in the school. I use the work of Cummins (1986) as a template for looking at four major strands of instructional intervention. For the purposes of writing this monograph I have separated issues of instruction (chapter 4) from issues of staffing (chapter 5). Obviously, in real life schools do not divide in such a neat manner; personnel and school program and programming interact and influence each other. Under 'Pedagogy' I examine teaming and theming, the use of learning centres and small-group instruction, and grouping of students; under 'Cultural and Linguistic Incorporation' I look at the Inuit culture and perspective as well as the use of Inuktitut in the school; under 'Collaboration with the Community' I examine parental involvement, the school breakfast program (also further discussed in chapter 5, 'Staffing') and under 'Assessment' I look at the issue of the evaluation and tracking of students. It will be obvious to the reader that these interventions do not fit easily into separate categories and that the relationship between the interventions is interactive and dynamic. It became apparent as I wrote this chapter that there are two streams to this monograph. One stream is that of interventions that would be appropriate for any small, rural, North American school affected by poverty and the despair that accompanies it. The other stream deals with interventions that would be appropriate for a school in a minority cultural and linguistic position and deals with culture and empowerment. The reader should be aware of the two streams and may want to attend more to one than the other depending on his or her personal context.

Pedagogy

I should begin this chapter with a definition of program and programming, since a great deal of the chapter looks at these issues. Program is the body of knowledge, the content, that the children learn in school. Program is 'what' we teach. It is the vehicle through which the skills/concepts/attitudes of the curriculum are taught. Piniaqtavut (explained in the next section, Theming) tried to bring more relevant, Inuit-based program content to Nunavut schools. Programming refers to the strategies and approaches to create effective pedagogy. I use the term programming to mean the 'how' of teaching. Piniaqtavut also advocated certain programming strategies such as 'hands-on' learning, 'language across the curriculum,' and small-group instruction. In order to improve learning in schools, I felt that both program and programming had to be addressed. Simply providing material in Inuktitut is not sufficient to improve learning if that material is taught in a way that does not respect students' needs. And simply providing small-group discussion around material that is far removed from the students' experience will probably not lead to effective learning either. Program and programming influence each other and are intricately linked to teacher development.

One of the most striking things I remember when I arrived in Anurapaktuq was the wide range in the quality of program and programming being offered in different classes in the school. There was one class where an educator who believed in a child-centred approach to education was teaching. In this class the activities in which children were involved were purposeful and meaningful. The first language and culture of the children were respected and pervaded the whole class program. There was a variety of teaching methods used, from small-group instruction, to individual tasks at learning centres, to large-group discussions and sharing. In this class the children were generally engaged in learning and the tone of the class was one of respect for all individuals in the class. Consequently, children were generally on-task and the approach to discipline was proactive, so the teacher did not have to spend valuable class time 'dealing with discipline.' Basically, children in this class were enjoying school as it was intended to be – a place for learning and for having fun.

At the other end of the spectrum was another class with another educator. Here language (either Inuktitut or English) was taught as a separate subject rather than being a vehicle through which to teach concepts. There was little reading and writing in either language. The program was disjointed and subjects were taught in isolated segments.

The programming was also weak; essentially the only teaching strategy used was the transmission method to the whole group. There was almost no individualization for different students' needs. Because the needs of the students were not being met, many students were off-task and the teacher spent a large part of what should have been 'learning' time dealing with discipline 'problems,' and there was generally a punitive tone to the class. The children in this class were not meeting the goals of schooling – many weren't learning much and most were not having 'fun.'

The rest of the classes fell somewhere between these two ends of the spectrum, with the majority of classes being more like the latter than the former. The challenge for me as principal was to know how to make instruction more consistently child-centred and interactive – how to change the type of instruction in classes where only the transmission method was being used so that in every class the needs of each child were being met. I think this ought to be the challenge for any principal – to ensure that the needs of all the children are being met. Principals are very aware that such 'islands of good pedagogy' exist in a school. There are some classes a principal would love to see his or her own child enter and others where a principal would not be overjoyed to put his or her child. The challenge for me was to learn how to spread the good pedagogy throughout all classes in the school.

In one way, trying to describe the effective programming strategies that turned Anurapaktuq School into a place where kids were learning and enjoying school is a bit like taking apart a puzzle. To examine one piece alone does not give one an idea of what the whole looks like, yet each piece is necessary in order to have an understanding of the whole. No one intervention on its own could have produced the effects that we saw over four years; often the interventions were very interdependent. For example, teaming came about almost as a consequence of theme planning. Small-group instruction required teaming and influenced the development of centres. The cultural base of the school was enhanced by theme planning and recruiting more Inuit staff. For the purpose of this chapter, I will try to separate each of the strands mentioned above and look at them in detail, but in the end the reader must realize that to understand the total school picture these strands must be interwoven.

Theming

In 1987 there were two major trends occurring in the NWT that helped to give us direction in the area of programming. The first was a focus on a 'language across the curriculum' approach. This approach advocated that all teachers, in all subject areas, were language teachers, and that language development should take place in subjects besides traditional language arts. The second trend was that of using theme planning in Baffin classrooms. The development of Piniaqtavut – an initiative to include an Inuit perspective in the school program – was guided by the work of Cummins (1986) on empowering minority students. Piniaqtavut advocated the use of the standard skills and concepts outlined by the Northwest Territories School Curriculum, but provided a program of study that would be more relevant to Baffin students. The content of Piniaqtavut would be more related to the everyday lives and experiences of Inuit students and, wherever possible, would be developed from an Inuit perspective. Most important for our work in Anurapaktuq, Piniaqtavut advocated a thematic approach to teaching. For each grade level several core themes were chosen that would be appropriate for Baffin students. Each theme could last anywhere from two to six weeks, depending on the grade level and interest of the students. Some material for these themes would be developed centrally at the Baffin Divisional Board of Education's Center for Teaching and Learning, such as was done with the themes of polar bears and dog teams. However, some themes would be developed at the community level as teachers explored community knowledge.

I remember as a consultant in 1985 going into a school where a new southern teacher was working on her long-range plans for the year, as requested by her principal. She had photocopied all the major curriculum documents, had cut up all the concepts and skills she was supposed to teach, and was fitting the little pieces into a large yearly calendar. For example, she was filling January with the science skills of teaching weather, social studies with a study of circumpolar peoples, math with the teaching of fractions, health with the study of disease prevention, and language arts with a novel study. Not only was this approach to the program very disjointed (exposing children to many different concepts all at once); her real problem came at the end of her exercise. Each month was jam-packed with as many concepts and skills as possible, and yet, at the end of the exercise, she was left with (literally) a whole fistful of skills and concepts that she could not fit into her year. Luckily, when she asked her smart supervisor of schools what to do in such a case, the wise woman responded by taking her over to the garbage can and dumping the excess into the garbage. 'You can only teach what you have time to teach!'

Unfortunately, not all teachers were lucky to have such wise counsel. Teachers in many Nunavut classrooms, under the pressure of teaching all the curriculum, often in a second-language situation, try to ram content and skills into students without allowing the necessary time for students to really learn. Unless it is clearly articulated both at the board and the school level that education is to be child-centred, teachers fall into the trap of owing more allegiance to the curriculum content than to the needs of the students.

And so, for many students, learning becomes difficult and less relevant, and consequently for teachers it becomes harder and harder to 'control' the class and handle the discipline problems, which result from program that is not relevant or meaningful. The teacher then starts an endless cycle of trying to manage children who are misbehaving because the program is not interesting or engaging enough and the programming is ineffective.[1] A cycle of misbehaviour by the students and punishing by the teacher begins that makes school fun for no one.

From an educational point of view teaching using themes makes a great deal of sense. Rather than teaching several, often unrelated, subjects in one day, subjects are reorganized so that there is an integration of different disciplines and more continuity throughout the child's day. Students learn in a holistic rather than a disjointed fashion.[2] Language is not separated into an isolated chunk, but pervades all subject areas and becomes the medium for instruction.

In the first classroom noted at the beginning of this chapter I made reference to a teacher who embodied everything that Piniaqtavut espoused, although she had not been involved in its development. Her good, sound pedagogy happened to coincide with that advocated by Piniaqtavut. My concern was how to get the other five classes in the school to emulate that class. As long as each of the five was doing a program that was different from any other, it meant that if I as a principal wanted to influence program and instruction in the school, I would have to do the same job of sitting and planning with teachers five times a day. At first that is what I tried to do. I was able to convince a couple of teachers to plan out their year in a thematic way, which meant that there was more integration of subjects within a class. That indeed was an improvement from teaching isolated, separate subjects.

As a first step that was not a bad place to start. The exemplary teacher offered a workshop to other staff on the logistics of how to actually go about theme planning. This beginning step of having people in their own classroom teach through themes had important implications for the Inuktitut program in the senior part of the school.

Ooleepeeka was the Inuktitut instructor for Grades 4 to 9, and she would spend forty minutes each day per class teaching Inuktitut. In most cases it meant that she would read a bit from one of the ten books available in Inuktitut at the time, tell a story to the students, and then have a wordsearch or puzzle for the students to complete. These classes were frustrating for students and for Ooleepeeka, who often had to spend a lot of her time dealing with student misbehaviour. When we began to have southern teachers use themes in the senior classes, it meant that there was something for Ooleepeeka to hinge her program on. I remember that one of the first themes the older students did was caribou. It allowed them to explore life functions in science using caribou as a basis. Very importantly, it allowed Ooleepeeka to have a topic around which she could develop a program. She certainly knew a lot about caribou! Ooleepeeka and I and a bilingual teacher were then able, in a one-hour planning period each week, to plan activities and ideas that Ooleepeeka could use with the students over the course of the theme. These planning sessions also allowed us time to help Ooleepeeka develop better and more varied programming skills. Never before had anyone had the time to sit and train her in the art of teaching. Ooleepeeka was able to learn lots of whole-language strategies, which she then used in Inuktitut.[3] It was a huge breakthrough for the way in which Inuktitut was taught and perceived in the school. Instead of merely doing puzzles, the students actually started reading and writing about real things in Inuktitut. (I had noticed by looking at the students' work, and it was confirmed by both the Inuit staff and the students, that most of the older students felt uncomfortable writing in Inuktitut and had seldom been asked to write anything more than a sentence throughout their school careers. However, with persistence and encouragement and good pedagogy we saw amazing growth in even three months.)

For the first three or four months, as we all got our feet under us and tried to come to know the children and the community, this approach of individual teachers doing themes in their classes worked well enough. However, there was still a great deal of difference in the quality of instruction among the different classrooms. And in Inuktitut Ooleepeeka was offering four different programs to four different classes. All this took a lot of planning and preparation time on everyone's part. Our real breakthrough in program came in February of our first year when I and a teacher on staff who was using themes were able to get several classes together to do a theme. We decided to chose a theme that would have high interest to our students and not worry so much about how much of the NWT curriculum concepts/skills/content it actually dealt with. At the time, wrestling was big in Anurapaktuq and we decided that we would use that as a theme. Our Community Education Council gave us permission to have an early dismissal at 2:30 each Thursday, and during that early closing we came together to brainstorm as many activities as we could on a wrestling theme. We tried to find activities that would encourage language and be fun for the students. We thought of different pieces of literature or songs that we could use or adapt to suit the theme. We thought of any science, health, social-studies, or math concepts that we could teach through wrestling. We thought of activities that we could do between and among classes from kindergarten to Grade 9 that would encourage big and little students to work together.

What the wrestling theme did for us as a staff was break the feeling of islands in the school – the feeling of unconnectedness from one class to another.[5] It really brought people together in a sense of team – a sense of sharing and of professional collegiality.[6] It allowed less experienced teachers to watch the way more experienced teachers plan and think out activities and to learn from that modelling. By the end of the session we had brainstormed activities that could be used throughout the school, but more importantly we had made joint decisions about how much writing we hoped for, how much reading and of what kind we wanted students to do, and how many learning centres we hoped for in each room.[7] We also learned that sharing the task made less work for any one person and that the kinds of ideas generated by eight or ten heads are better than those thought up by a single teacher. It allowed me as principal to have direct influence on the kinds of ideas that were being reinforced – 'Yes, that's great. Let's get more letter writing going.' – and it allowed me to see where the planning process was going.

Later if I went into a class I would be able to get an idea of the direction in which the class was going. By being involved at the grass-roots level I was also made aware of the areas where we needed more resources, materials, or in-service.

Our first school-wide theme was a hit! The students responded beautifully to it, producing more writing that we had ever anticipated. (How could you be eleven years old and live in Anurapaktuq and *not* have an opinion on who is better – Hulk Hogan or Jake the Snake?) People got into the habit of sharing materials and ideas and placing those ideas in an idea box for all to share. Ooleepeeka could do lots of activities related to traditional Inuit wrestling and tests of strength, and she didn't have to plan five separate different programs. There also evolved a strange sort of accountability for programs and themes among the staff and students. For one thing, students' writing in English and Inuktitut was plastered over the school and the expectation that every student can write something began to evolve. In terms of staff, sharing common themes allowed them to compare activities among themselves. If one activity went well in one class and bombed in another the staff was able to look at their teaching style to see if that might influence how the activity went. Doing a school-wide theme also provided many natural occasions for students to work cooperatively. Older students could be writing the books from which younger students would read (especially important since there were still few Inuktitut books at the time). Older students also realized that they were modelling for younger students and they seemed to take pride in their work. During this school-wide theme what was primarily shared was activities related to language arts. And that was a manageable bite for the first theme. We didn't try to get people doing centres or sharing math groups or changing their method of evaluation at that point. It was enough that they had decided to theme together.

With the success of that theme the staff decided to try more themes together. We approached the Community Education Council to have an early closing twice a month, during which the staff could meet and plan themes together. These biweekly meetings became important staff in-service events, because during each meeting we were talking about teaching and pedagogy. People began to see the connection between behaviour and programming and to see that the more relevant the program, the more individualized and varied the programming, the less reason students had to misbehave. These planning sessions became an important arena in which to influence the direction of change in the school.[8]

Our first year we continued with themes from February to May. We often did themes by division (K–3 would share a theme and 4–9 would share a theme), but we did do a couple more school-wide themes. We had to chose school-wide themes that were broader to allow teachers and students freedom to go off in their own directions. At the end of our first year teachers were pleased with the common-theme approach, and we decided to plan ahead for the themes for our second year in June of 1987. Staff turnover was very low, with only two teachers leaving, so we were able to have good continuity into the next year. We chose some themes from Piniaqtavut, some based on teacher interest, and some based on areas of science, social studies, or health that we felt had been neglected in the past. By choosing our themes in advance we were able to order our school materials more effectively. One of the initial problems that teachers encounter when they start sharing themes is that there aren't enough materials for all classes to share. Certainly it doesn't make it easy if you're doing dinosaurs and there are only three books on dinosaurs in the whole school. Some minimal resource material is required. However, by using a whole-language approach much of the material can be generated by the students themselves, and what really needs to be shared then are teacher ideas and construction materials. It was definitely easier each year that we continued with themes because we were able to keep building up the resources in our school theme boxes. We continued over four years with the pattern of doing some school-wide themes – about one of every five themes is school-wide; and it helps to build up school spirit and staff solidarity. Throughout my time in the community themes were chosen on the basis of teacher interest, suggestions from Piniaqtavut, and the requirements of NWT curriculum, but beginning in 1989 we began asking for student input and then chose some themes on student interest. We hoped that this trend would continue as students took a more active role in what they were learning.

By 1991 the process of theme planning had become fairly routine in the school. A group of educators would get together on an afternoon when there was an early dismissal. Before coming to a theme planning session each teacher had looked at the skills and concepts that he or she hoped to cover in that theme. (This selection of skills/concepts for each theme took place in a group planning session.) So, for example, if the theme is rockets, the teacher may have decided that he or she would teach about states of matter in science, linear measurement in math, and effects of technology on culture in social studies and health. As well as having the skill/concepts selected for the theme, each teacher would have thought a bit about the theme before the meeting in order to bring a few ideas for activities. As principal and Program Support Teacher I would have thought about the theme and have started to collect some resource material and placed it in a 'theme box.' At the actual theme planning meeting, then, for about an hour the group would brainstorm ideas, activities, and special projects that could be done during the theme. A secretary recorded all the ideas. People would have a copy of the skills/concepts/attitudes they hoped to cover during the teaching of a theme, and with an eye on those they tried to think of activities or ideas that would cover the specific content. Without reference to the skills/concepts/attitudes one hopes to cover, it is very easy to go off on spirals in a theme and have a lot of fun, but never cover any formal curriculum material. It was always a real balancing act to include the formal curriculum material but not let it dictate the whole theme such that the theme became a series of skills and the spontaneity that comes from interactive teaching became lost. (Balancing the needs of the formal requirements of the curriculum with the needs and interests of the student is an ever-present tension in education, and in my mind requires constant reflection, evaluation, and re-evaluation. In far too many cases, formal requirements of curriculum are imposed upon students without taking into consideration the prior knowledge, experience, and interests the student may possess.) Once the brainstorming was complete, each teacher chose from the generated list of activities and ideas – the 'menu' – those activities and ideas that he or she would like to do with students and copied down those ideas on his or her theme sheet. This sheet would be the reference chart for the whole theme and it was from here that the teacher would break the theme further down into daily activities in the plan book. I explain this process in detail in a previous publication (Tompkins 1991).[9]

Beginning in 1989, through a cooperative effort with the Community Education Council, a special outdoor program was offered to students in the late spring. By creative scheduling we were able to have half of the teachers participate in the outdoor program during the first week. The other half stayed in school and began working on their long-range theme planning for the next year, and actually planned out their first theme for August before they left for summer holidays. (In the second week of the program the two groups flip-flopped). This procedure of doing planning in advance greatly helped new staff members coming to the school and also allowed staff to be ready to start programs right away in the fall. In addition, the principal could be sure that materials for the themes were ordered over the summer months.

Being involved in the planning kept the principal's job 'educational' for me. Too often people leave 'education' to become principals. Most of what they end up doing in their job becomes removed from the task of helping people develop as professionals. By being involved in the planning and programming I inevitably became involved in instruction. I was involved in the challenge of translating curriculum into meaningful programming, and very involved in trying to help staff members become more skilled teachers.[10] Sometimes this meant actually showing a staff member, through modelling, how to use math manipulatives. Sometimes it actually meant team teaching with a teacher who was unsure of how to present a certain topic to children or needed help with managing a group of children. I was able to remember just how much time planning and preparation takes for good teachers.[11] As a result of being proactive with the staff I was able to avoid the many things that draw principals away from classrooms – student discipline problems, community complaints, or staff discipline problems – and turn them into administrators and evaluators rather than instructional leaders. Through good, sound planning and follow-up support provided in the classroom most students were having their needs met. Therefore, the students were happier and more on-task in class, their parents were happier with their successes, and teachers were being reinforced both by the students' motivation and achievement and by colleague and principal acknowledgment.[12]

Teaming

Looking back, it almost seems like teaming was a natural by-product of theme planning. In many ways I think that is true. As I've already stated, it's almost impossible not to start reaching a feeling of being a team when you are planning together, sharing successes and frustrations, and even making materials for each other to use in classrooms. People start to develop a sense of rowing in the same direction, of wanting the same things for students, and they do start to see they have a bigger responsibility than just to the kids in their own classroom. They begin to see that each teacher has a role to play in making the school a safe and happy learning environment for all the children. The biweekly planning sessions offered people the chance to support each other in very real ways, and this went a long way in creating a sense of team. There were, however, in the beginning some overt steps taken to create that sense of team. In the first year a lot of work was done on goal setting as a staff so that people could at least agree on the direction of the school. In order for people to have a sense of team, they must have some sense of sharing a vision. One of the first meetings that I facilitated with the staff in August of 1987 sought to develop a mission statement with staff and then list objectives and measures for the goals we had set. This mission statement and goals were later shared with and supported by the Community Education Council. Creating the mission statement was important in providing us with a common direction and aim, which in itself reinforced the concept of team and 'rowing the same way.'

Weekly in-service (see chapter 5) allowed the staff a chance to come together and focus on staff development. Some of the earliest in-services involved specific group activities to encourage cooperation between staff members and allow people to reflect on team building. Some such activities included learning Inuit songs as a group, publishing books together, and sharing art ideas.

Working as part of a team brought educators down to a level of honesty that is not easily reached in most traditional school settings. People could talk about programming, and as they did frustrations would come up and become the basis of further discussion. These frustrations did not come up in the form of a complaint session, but rather as people talked – for example, about the difficulty of getting children to write; other teachers could offer suggestions or the whole staff could come to the agreement that we needed more in-service on how to get kids to write. I think that since I was spending time in each classroom each week working with children, I earned a certain credibility as 'being in the trenches' with the teachers, as being a fellow educator, and I felt that teachers did not feel under the pressure of being evaluated at these planning sessions.[13] By comments I got from teachers over the four years I felt that they saw these sessions as opportunities for professional growth and sharing. The stronger, more experienced educators got a chance to share some of their ideas and successes – there's nothing a teacher enjoys doing more. These teachers also had the opportunity to model and almost become 'teacher trainers' for other teachers on staff. Because other, less experienced staff members were pleased at the real support they were receiving, they gave good feedback to the stronger teachers. Almost immediately a feeling of goodwill and team spirit began to develop among the whole staff.[14] There was a sense of the programming being a shared responsibility and not a feeling of people 'stealing' other people's ideas or always relying on the stronger teachers. New and less experienced teachers who went through the biweekly planning sessions began to see the patterns – how activities could be used from one theme to the next – and began to grow in their knowledge of planning.

Initially people teamed up in the planning sessions and then went off and prepared materials on their own. As time went on, teachers began to team together to make materials for group use. Later on, when we started small-group instruction, people began to team teach in each other's classrooms and with expressive-arts groups. All of these activities brought people together and put them into situations where they had to cooperate. As with any new skill, many of us had to learn how to be good team members. There were certainly times when each of us failed in some way or another – when we were insensitive, when we didn't follow through on what we said we'd do – and I'm sure there were days in the beginning when we thought it would be easier to go back to teaching alone! However, given the opportunity to support and give feedback to each other, I think I would be safe in saying that no staff member at the school would want to go back to doing it alone. More heads and hands have meant better programs for kids in the school.

As a principal I feel strongly that being involved at the planning level of program implementation was one of my most important roles. As I see it, most principal intervention is reactive, not proactive. Principals go in to observe a lesson, usually without having seen where the lesson fits into the whole program. If it's a good lesson, given by an experienced educator, we generally give feedback, walk out of the room, and wish that all classes in the school were like this one. If it's a poor lesson, we usually try to pick one or two areas, like presentation of material or classroom management, then start in the middle trying to improve the situation. It may in fact have been at the planning level that the lesson failed. Perhaps the material is not relevant, perhaps nothing appears integrated to the students, perhaps the teacher is relying solely on a particular activity or teaching strategy. By being present at the planning session the principal is able to come face to face with the realities the teachers are facing as they plan.[15] Perhaps this is why many principals avoid becoming involved. It requires as much risk taking on the part of the principal as it does on the part of the staff. Sometimes in Anurapaktuq we realized that we simply didn't have enough resources to teach a certain topic, or that we couldn't think of ways to present material in an understandable fashion. This most often occurred when we were working with the program conducted primarily in Inuktitut.

Learning Centres

In my work in helping to mainstream students with special needs into regular classes I found that one of the most useful tools to help facilitate individualization for students was learning centres. If a teacher can accept having small groups of regular students work on different activities at the same time, it is much easier for the teacher to see a student with special needs working on a different activity. In a classroom where the whole class is always expected to do the same activity at the same time, it is very hard to individualize the teaching for different learning needs.

Early in the first year in Anurapaktuq I tried to encourage the use of learning centres. What I found was that until people had really started looking at the total program and started theme planning, it was difficult to know what kind of centres to set up and how to run them. It also became clear that most educators needed training in using learning centres. Thus, only late in our second year were centres implemented school-wide. Centres provided teachers with an important way of individualizing work for students and of allowing students to work independently. Anurapaktuq students became capable of working independently, and in 1989 one of the school review team members, the principal of Cape Dorset, noted how independent the older students were during centre time. On several occasions teachers from Anurapaktuq were invited to present workshops to other schools and regional teachers' conferences on the use of learning centres.

I had begun exploring centres myself as a teacher in Pangnirtung and learned a lot more from a very experienced teacher on the Anurapaktuq staff who had learned about them while in England. She made my job of getting centres started easier because she actually had them working in her class, so I could bring other teachers there and allow her to model their use. I learned two important things about centres during my time in Anurapaktuq. The first was that centres worked best when they were integrated as part of the theme; the second was that most teachers needed help getting centres started and maintaining them once they had begun.

Often teachers embrace the ideas very readily and start off trying to set up fifteen interesting, engaging, learning centres each week in a class. They are often unable to keep up with the preparation time required to implement such a program, and after a few weeks centres are no longer used. In an attempt to encourage learning centres in all classes and to provide the support necessary to keep them going on a long-term basis, brainstorming the possible activities for, and actually preparing, learning centres became part of our theme-planning sessions. Since many classes can be working on the same theme, it is possible to use many of the same ideas for various learning centres. Before the theme-planning meeting broke up, each person took the responsibility to create two or three learning-centre activities, but to make duplicates or triplicates of each activity so they could be shared with other classes. For example, if the listening-centre activity for a unit on whales was to have someone make a tape to go with a book on whales, that person would make three tapes and give one to each class in his or her division, along with instructions for that centre activity. In this way a single teacher is not left with the formidable task of planning and creating twelve or thirteen different centre activities for each theme. Left on their own most teachers cannot keep up with the work involved in preparing student learning centres. With this kind of team support the work is shared among six to eight people, and so we have managed to continue using learning centres as an important part of the school program. Since I was involved in the planning I was also available to make some centres for the theme. It has been our experience that the more hands-on math and art materials in a school, the wider the variety of activities that can be placed at learning centres. Nor do teachers have to make every centre from scratch. For example, manipulative math materials like pattern blocks, geoboards, and templates can be used throughout the school at learning centres. However, if they are not available in the school, or are in very limited supply, they can be of no help. By being involved in planning I began to have a better idea of the kinds of materials that we needed to be ordering for the school.

Small-Group Instruction

One of our goals in Anurapaktuq was to make the program meet the needs of each child. We knew that, as in any school, there was a wide variety of abilities in each class. We wanted to acknowledge, build upon, and celebrate these differences. We wanted to deal with this wide range in achievement positively, rather than simply complain about it. Most instruction in most classes was being done with the total group. Teachers did not feel comfortable teaching, or did not know how to teach, smaller groups. Some teachers felt that the students did not have the skills to work independently while they taught a small group; others felt unsure about how to supervise two or three groups at a time. In my role as principal I felt it was important for me to be in classrooms supporting teachers – not just dropping by once in a while on a 'walkabout.'

Being involved in the planning stage was probably the most important first step towards improving classroom instruction in the school. On a professional level it made people more conscious of how important and time-consuming the planning process is and how more heads make for more, and usually better, ideas at the planning stage. It served as a way of informally in-servicing staff on various areas of program. And it introduced people to the idea of working in a team. Great benefits, professional and personal, were developed from this experience, and people began to feel like they could share with and help each other. But to actually improve instruction at the classroom level it was never enough to just talk about it. People needed help in the classroom itself.

The area that I felt comfortable starting in small-group instruction was mathematics, but we later expanded the groups to include writing workshops and expressive arts. I had taken courses in using a manipulative approach to teaching math (Mathematics Their Way) and I found that most teachers felt comfortable being able to break down math skills. Initially, I would go into a class and work with the teacher. The teacher would take a group of eight students, I would take a group of eight students, and eight students would be working out of their math books or workbooks. After twenty minutes each group would rotate, so that during an hour each student had two instructional sessions and had done some independent seat work. We came to call this set-up 'supported math groups,' and it was almost invariably and instantly a success! Because we were working with eight students it was very easy to see the functioning level of the student, and since 'management' was not an issue it was possible to do lots of interesting and fun things that teachers don't usually do in math with a whole class because they fear they will lose control. The students in those small teaching groups were engaged and were usually succeeding because instruction could be much more individualized. Teachers were able to learn how to break down skills, learn how to challenge students with problem-solving activities, learn ways to see that mastery of a given concept had occurred, learn how to record this learning on student progress charts, and learn to see that each student could be moving at a different rate. The group at the independent table was learning as much about working independently without the supervision of a teacher as they were doing reinforcement work. The whole class was learning how to work with a higher noise level and how to tune the other groups out and stay on task.[17]

I was not the only staff member who did small-group support. Other staff members were able to offer the same support to other classes through creative timetabling. All teachers, including the physical-education specialist, were involved in supporting math groups.

As a result of this team teaching we began to share more ideas and to learn more about strategies for teaching math. In our planning meetings we would look at our math skills and often pick common math strands to cover during a theme. On the one hand, we tried to pick math content that might naturally fit with a theme topic. For example, in covering a wrestling theme one could choose to study mass in math and compare body weights of wrestlers, express those weights in grams and kilograms, or convert kilograms to pounds. By having several teachers choose that 'strand' of mass, which runs through the math program from K–9, multiple activities could be created and shared across grades. In a short ten-minute brainstorming session at one of these meetings we could brain-storm sixteen different ways to teach mass and share teaching strategies. We looked at how manipulatives can be used throughout the school from K–9. Again, it becomes apparent how the planning sessions also served as a forum for staff development and in-service on an on-going basis. As we planned our math program together we shared ideas about math teach-ing and started keeping idea folders on every math concept we taught, so that after two or three years we had huge folders of games and ideas that could be used to teach fractions from K–9. We learned about manage-ment issues related to group work – how to track where the students are and how to control movement in the class. We also began to see where we needed more materials, and as a result concentrated on building up our math manipulatives in the school. We bought teaching videos to help us learn better ways to teach certain concepts. Through an arrangement with Arctic College another teacher and I were given permission to offer a Background Math course in the evenings to our teacher trainees to have them learn more about math and gain credits towards their certi-fication.

During the first year we tried to have supported math groups in all classes, but only managed to have them in three classes. During the second and third year, by juggling staff around and using everyone, we managed to have supported math groups in each class each day. In our fourth year, with the addition of a principal-in-training position and more creative timetabling, we had three teachers instead of two team teaching in math classes, so that children were receiving all their math instruction in small groups.

The effect that this had on teachers and students and on math in-struction was very significant. For teachers it meant they had the luxury of really seeing the effect of their instruction. This had later implications for evaluation and tracking. Usually, in a class of twenty-five most teachers can't really see whether a student has learned or not. By working with small groups one can see how students are learning, where confusion is occurring, and how to move on to the next step. Because the teaching is better (the teacher can see the effectiveness of his or her teaching and modify and adjust as he or she goes along), the students are relaxed and challenged and able to work at tasks that are appropriate to their ability. Problems related to being off-task and to fear of failure seem to disappear and the teacher/student relationship improves greatly. The number of be-haviour problems and parental complaints dropped greatly from my first year in Anurapaktuq to subsequent years, and I cannot help but feel that students simply began to be more successful as the years went on.[18] Student self-esteem usually improves because they are having a great deal of success and school is becoming a place where they can learn and are having fun. Then, because the students are more relaxed, the teacher relaxes more, and this in turn causes the students to relax and be more cooperative, and a wonderful cycle of learning happens. This is not to suggest that there weren't days when we had to prod the odd individual along, but generally students were very on-task during math and teachers found this a productive, and usually an enjoyable, period. Teachers came to understand the relationship between program and behaviour problems. When a student is challenged at his or her level, there are seldom problems of misbehaviour. Both the teacher and the students are also learning the skills of independent learning. Students are learning to work on their own, to work while another group is playing a game, to ask peers for help rather than running to the teacher, and teachers are learning to accept that students can all be at different levels and using different materials.

I truly believe that until teachers have experienced the delight of teaching a small group they haven't really understood very much about the teaching act. My experience has been that once the students are able to learn in situations where the teacher is not hovering over them, they are much more able to work independently at learning centres, or in small writing groups, and be on-task.[19] They become more responsible because they are having to deal with responsibility. Comments from visitors in our school would always include statements about how on-task the students were and how they could be left to work on their own in the library or at the computer and would not just 'fool around.' Once teachers had learned how to use small groups in math period, then they were less fearful to move into group work for writing or for science.

As principal, I enjoyed the math instruction myself because it gave me a real reason to be in the classroom. First of all, it kept me involved in teaching, which is something that I enjoy and the reason I became a teacher. I could learn a lot about the teacher's style of management and help provide support where needed. By being in the classroom I got to know almost all the students in the school in a very personal way, and I was challenged to continually work at improving my own teaching skills. I was more likely to empathize with the frustrations that teachers felt when students were too tired to work or arrived late or simply were not motivated to learn. I always felt that by being in the classroom I kept my feet on the ground and rooted in reality! It also gave me a chance to model instruction for teachers when necessary and to do it on site.

Later we used small-group instruction to help improve writing in the school, and it proved to be a very important support for students. We also used small-group instruction in our expressive arts program.

Grouping of Students

In 1987 there did not seem to be a standard policy or practice to help guide teachers in the placement of students in grades. This is not surprising, since teacher turnover had been high, most teachers worked in relative isolation from one another, and there was little opportunity to discuss such educational issues school-wide. In 1987 the groupings of students was very uneven. In some cases it appeared to be done by age, in other cases by ability.[20] At the junior and intermediate end of the school, where poor attendance and poor instruction were catching up with students, there appeared to be many older students placed with younger students. Some older students were kept back with younger students because of their perceived weakness in English. The consequences of these placements were usually poor, as the older students often lost their self-confidence away from their peer group, then either dropped out of school or stayed in school and became behaviour problems.

By 1987 the Baffin Divisional Board had a policy which stated that students should be educated in a regular classroom with their same-age peers. My experience had shown that holding children back in school did not usually lead to future success. In fact, children were more likely to drop out of school if they were held back. During the first year we began to address the needs of students through better program planning and delivery and small-group instruction. These measures in themselves started to address some of the needs of these students who had repeated grades. In our second year, when we had a more stable staff and had begun to know the students, we attempted to group students more by age and peer group and not by ability. As a staff, the more we learned techniques of individualizing, such as learning centres and small-group instruction, the more the academic and social needs of the students were met. By the third year we began to realize that perhaps diversity was a good thing and we deliberately began to have classes with a wide variety of ages. In the third year, instead of having a Grade 7 class with all the thirteen-year-olds and a Grade 5/6 class with all the eleven- and twelve-year-olds, we made two classes of 5/6/7 so there were mixtures of students in each class. There were students who were doing well in ESL and those who were having difficulty. There were mature thirteen-year-olds and mature eleven-year-olds in each class. There were immature thirteen-year-olds and immature eleven-year-olds in each class. Consideration was given to the importance of peers, so that each student was sure to have at least one or two close friends in each class.

The school had also developed an expressive arts program, where students from Grade 4 to 9 were mixed up randomly into small groups of between ten and twelve students. Each teacher and other support staff members (myself, the physical-education teacher, teacher trainees who were available, and some community volunteers) took a group for two 45-minute time blocks each week for a six-week period and did an expressive activity with the students. The activities included model kayak building, knitting, doll making, cooking, bookmaking, guitar, and many others, and their purpose was to expand the curriculum to include a wider range of practical-art/fine-art activities. Students and teachers generally enjoyed this program immensely and a great deal of creative work was produced. From a grouping point of view it allowed the teachers to work with students of a variety of ages and abilities and get to know more students in a personal way. I think expressive arts helped teachers to see that mixed groups are probably a more accurate reflection of the way people group themselves outside of school. In Anurapaktuq children of mixed ages usually played together.

The full actualization of this reasoning was implemented in 1991 when 'family groupings' were started in the school as a result of discussion that came out of the school review. Several of the board consultants felt that the school in Anurapaktuq was well along the road to individualizing instruction for students and that family grouping represented a next logical step for the direction of the school. Board staff had given us some articles to read on the use of mixed ability groupings and we had heard (but saw no literature) that this practice was used with native children in New Zealand. Family groupings seemed to reinforce a practice that was occurring naturally in Anurapaktuq, where older children were often responsible for and cared for, as well as enjoyed and played with, younger children.

In the family groupings model children are deliberately mixed up by age in a class. In a real family, children are of varying ages, yet they all learn from one another as well as from their parents. So in family-grouped classrooms, students are expected to learn from those older and younger than themselves. In the primary end of the school, in 1991 there were three classrooms. In each classroom there were some kindergarten students, some Grade 1 students, some Grade 2 students, and some Grade 3 students. The students ranged in age from five to ten years old. Groupings in family-grouped classrooms were fluid and constantly changing depending on the needs of the class. A Grade 2 student might be working with some older students during math time because he was ready to learn multiplying, whereas in language he might be working with younger students who are still working on simple pattern stories. More mature students in family-grouping classes become helpers and will peer-teach fellow students. Diversity by age, size, and ability becomes accepted. Each class had between twenty-five and twenty-seven students and two Inuit staff members (combination of teachers, teacher-trainees, and special-needs assistants). During math time and writing time there was additional support.

In the middle of the school the classes were grouped in a similar fashion: there was a 4/5/6 classroom, a 5/6/7 classroom, and a 7/8/9 classroom. These classes differed from the traditional multi-grade classes (which often result from a lack or surplus of students in a particular grade) in that no attempt was made to keep the Grade 4's sitting together and different from the Grade 5's.

The effect of these family groupings was felt by both teachers and students. Teachers began to really individualize teaching for students. Again, since small-group instruction, team teaching, and learning centres were in place, it was much easier to look at each child and determine the level at which the child was functioning, then teach at that level. Family grouping helped teachers to move away from the idea of students being in a grade. Too often teachers will look at a child and say, 'Oh, he's only in Grade 2 – he can't start division' or 'He's in Grade 5 – he must know multiplication.' We all began to realize that in math a fourteen-year-old may know fractions really well, but may still be struggling with carrying and borrowing. She may be excellent in math, but be only a beginning reader. To assign a number to students, like Grade 5, somehow averages out to a meaningless concept. Family groupings really helped teachers to start to achieve true individualization for each student. Grouping students like this forced us as a staff to move to a continuous evaluation process rather than a graded system.[21]

For the students, family grouping modelled itself after what happens in the family and the community. In Anurapaktuq most older children were responsible for a great deal of the care and training of their younger siblings. In play situations it was not uncommon to see children of very mixed ages playing together – much more common than in southern Canada. Family groupings gave children the chance to be together in groups that were not based on how smart you were in math or reading. They helped reinforce the concept that everybody is good at different things, everybody needs help at some point, and everybody can be a helper at some point. Many of the children came from families that were in great turmoil, and they had great emotional needs. Allowing these children to be helpers went a long way, I think, to increasing their feeling of self-worth.

Family groupings also helped reinforce the notion that school is more than just a place to learn. It is also a place to have fun with your friends and look after them. Caring became an important ingredient in these classes; students learned that relationships – how people treat each other – are just as important as scoring 100 on your math test. In a community struck tragically by eight suicides in eight years (1983–91) the value of taking care of others cannot be overestimated (LeChat 1991).

Cultural and Linguistic Incorporation

Theming and teaming seemed to address many of the problems related to programming, resource development, and teacher development, but it was a challenge to create a truly Inuit perspective in the school, particularly when in 1987 the principal was non-Inuit, as I was, and the majority of the educators were non-Inuit. To create an Inuit school, then, our first goal had to be to attract and train more Inuit staff. All of the interventions mentioned previously could lead to improved learning, but they could not lead to empowerment in the way Cummins (1986) intends it. I have chosen to devote the next chapter to a discussion of how the school developed from having a majority of Qallunaaq educators in 1987 to having a majority of Inuit educators in 1991.

I do, however, include a discussion of Inuit perspective, language, and culture in this chapter because there are interventions possible to enhance Inuit perspective, language, and culture even in situations where few Inuit staff are available in a school. One such intervention was the use of theme and team planning. An example from the teaching of science can illustrate how these pedagogical interventions could strengthen Inuktitut. Take, for example, a theme we were doing on snow. It seemed simple enough to suggest that we teach the states of matter as part of this theme. However, by sitting down and theme planning we (especially I) began to realize that many, many science concepts did not exist in Inuktitut in the ways that Qallunaaq see them or they have not yet been translated into Inuktitut. As a group, the Inuit staff had to come to an understanding of the concepts of the states of matter and then agree on a vocabulary to use in Inuktitut to explain those concepts. Some Inuit staff members have previously avoided teaching certain science concepts because there were no words for such concepts as energy, force, or electricity. It is true that the exact translatable word might not exist, but certainly these phenomena exist in the Inuit world, and so I felt that to keep Inuktitut a living, evolving language we had to help teachers and students be able to talk about these concepts in Inuktitut. If Inuktitut is not capable of describing both the traditional and the modern world, then it becomes doomed to be a language of the past. In some cases new words need to be invented, in other cases it is a matter of describing the concept in words and not having a single term. Within the forum of theme planning with teaming, such issues could arise and be discussed and worked through, and Inuit staff were able to teach more and more of the program in Inuktitut.

One of the goals of Piniaqtavut is to create schools that will better reflect the Inuit communities that they serve. It is hoped that more of Inuit perspective will come across through the study of topics that are more relevant to Inuit students. Previously in our school, and in many schools, 'Inuit culture' was viewed as a separate part of the school program. It was not uncommon for students to spend almost a whole day in class, often with a Qallunaaq teacher, studying the formal curriculum. They would leave class perhaps twice a week to go out and 'do Inuit culture' – often girls to sew slippers and boys to make harpoons. Or, as in the case of Ooleepeeka, an elder would come in and teach 'culture/ language' to the students as if they were static entities unto themselves. Such a view of culture/language is patronizing and treats both as if they were not living and vibrant, not 'real curriculum' or in any way meaningful to the present day.[22]

As previously mentioned, three important strategies led to Inuit culture becoming an integral part of the school program in Anurapaktuq. The first, which will be discussed in the next chapter, was increasing the number of Inuit educators in the school. The second was the use of theming and team planning to help support the present Inuit educators in their work. By creating the opportunity for staff to work together, by building a strong sense of team in which Inuit educators are seen as equal members of the staff, the Inuit perspective emerged. In 1987, Inuit staff were in the minority, but with team planning there were at least some Inuit around the table who could make contributions based on their experiences and beliefs. As the number of Inuit staff grew to the point where they became the majority of the staff, more discussion at the meetings took place in Inuktitut. Theme planning also helped to allow Inuit beliefs and attitudes to come through: the themes chosen were relevant to Inuit life and the activities and experiences chosen through which to teach the skills and concepts would be relevant to the students. Themes such as the walrus, drug and alcohol abuse, and the life of people in other Baffin communities deeply touch the lives of the students and teachers in the community.

The third intervention which strengthened perspective, language, and culture was the conscious effort by the staff to enhance the use and value of Inuktitut in the school. It was readily apparent in 1987 that Inuktitut was not strongly reinforced in the school. It was not used as a medium for instruction beyond Grade 1 and the Inuktitut program for junior and intermediate students was sadly lacking. The instructor, though a native speaker, had no teacher training and few materials to support any kind of a program. The children's attitude towards Inuktitut was poor and few had skills in reading and writing their first language.[23]

In the goal setting in-service held during a professional-development day in August 1987 one of the important goals the staff set was to raise the status of Inuktitut in the school and to strive to make children fluent in both Inuktitut and English. All Inuit staff felt that the Inuktitut program needed to be strengthened, and recent research in the area of whole language and first-language acquisition convinced us of the need to promote fluency in Inuktitut. On a symbolic level every effort was made to display Inuktitut throughout the school and to make it as visible as English throughout the building. That was an important step and one that many schools try, but unless the way in which Inuktitut is used in the classrooms and throughout the school changes, the hallway displays will have had little impact.

What was needed was to change the way in which Inuktitut was used in classrooms. As stated in the section on theming, an important step that led to the valuing of Inuktitut was theme planning, which created an avenue for the use of Inuktitut for meaningful purposes and an opportunity for an Inuit perspective to emerge in the entire school program. With the help of experienced staff members I was able to organize teacher training for teacher trainees to improve their overall language-instruction abilities and competency in Inuktitut. We were also able to benefit from the literature being published on whole language that described ways of making language (albeit usually English) more meaningful for students.[24] (This training was done as part of planning meetings, as part of staff in-service, and sometimes by freeing up Inuit staff to model for teacher trainees.) As part of staff in-service for the first two years we worked on learning and using whole-language techniques in both languages. Teachers and teacher trainees began to see Inuktitut as a language of instruction rather than simply a separate program. At the same time, the Baffin Divisional Board of Education was beginning to publish books in Inuktitut; and at the school level, older classes were starting to produce books in Inuktitut for students to read. Students throughout the whole school began to do journals in Inuktitut, there was Uninterrupted Sustained Silent Reading (USSR) in every class in Inuktitut, and teachers began to use ideas about the writing process in Inuktitut. Qallunaaq teachers were encouraged to set up USSR in Inuktitut, even though most of them could not read or speak in Inuktitut. Some Qallunaaq teachers used this time to practise their own reading in Inuktitut.

In the third year the school ordered several Macintosh computers so that students could produce their work in a more polished fashion. Reading and writing became important activities in every classroom from kindergarten to Grade 9. All classes participated in a buddy reading program in which older students read with younger ones in Inuktitut. In the third and fourth year all teachers team taught during writing periods to allow for more adult support in classrooms where children were beginning the writing process. Inuit educators would work together and Qallunaaq teachers would work together to improve writing in the school. Students were encouraged to submit writing in Inuktitut to Baffin board journals and contests. In 1990 the first- and third-place winners in the Inuit Circumpolar Conference Writing Competition were from our school.

The staff also agreed in August 1987 to try to speak more Inuktitut out of the classroom in the hallways, in the staff room, and all over the school. Inuit staff began to use more and more Inuktitut in planning and staff meetings. Qallunaaq staff were encouraged to greet students in Inuktitut and answer the phone in Inuktitut, and as a warm-up for in-services each Thursday all staff learned Inuit songs. The Qallunaaq staff learned varied amounts of Inuktitut depending on their length of stay in the community. Over the four-year period the majority of Qallunaaq teachers spent only two years in Anurapaktuq. Those staff who stayed longer developed more proficiency in Inuktitut, though none of us as non-Inuit staff would claim to be anywhere near fluent speakers.[25]

Over the four years the school attempted to use the tenets of whole language to create situations that would allow language to be used purposefully. We focused a great deal on reading and writing, especially in Inuktitut. USSR, teacher-read stories, and buddy reading became standard practices in all classes. Even in those classes lead by Qallunaaq these practices became standard through the use of staff teaming. All classes kept journals in Inuktitut (senior students alternated English and Inuktitut on different days). A school mailbox encouraged letter writing among students and teachers, and birthday cards and 'Thank you' cards were available to students. As part of the school program students were encouraged to write letters of concern to newspapers and politicians regarding topical issues. In addition, a school newsletter encouraged student writing. Writing became an important activity and students came to understood that everyone could be a writer.

We had to be much more deliberate about what we did in Inuktitut than we did in English. Even though Inuit are the majority in the Baffin, English is still the dominant language and with very little encouragement students will turn to English. This is not surprising when one considers that pop culture has reached the North and English is the language of pop culture. The key to encouraging more interest and pride in Inuktitut seemed to be to offer a good, solid, relevant program that would create a desire on the part of students to listen, speak, read, and write in their first language.[26]

Developing fluency became progressively easier over the four years as first-language skills were being more and more strengthened. Ireland (1990) has noted that students who had strong writing skills in Inuktitut carried those strong skills into English. Essentially, the staff used the same tenets of whole language to guide instruction in English. Having a wide variety of printed materials, putting students in situations where they had to communicate in English, and having relevant program and programming helped develop English fluency as well.

Collaboration with the Community

In 1987 the community felt distanced from the school. Cummins (1986) advocates that community involvement in the school helps to empower students. Community involvement is a two-way street – getting the community more into the school and getting the school and teachers more out into the community. In Anurapaktuq we developed several ways of getting the school more into the community. One simple procedure that we instituted from the start was to have teachers visit homes at least twice a year. Too often educators forget some of the difficult homes in which our students live and forget the emotional baggage they bring to school each day. This is certainly true for Qallunaaq teachers, who have the additional cultural bridge to cross, but even Inuit teachers felt that they could become removed from the reality certain students lived. Home visits served the important function of learning more about the family and the child and extending the school into the community. I made it a practice from my second year onward to do one or two home visits each week to drop off 'Good News' telegrams about students. I always felt these visits helped me enormously to extend myself into the community and use my Inuktitut.[27]

To help improve the relationship between the school and the community we concerned ourselves with improving student performance in school and getting more 'good news' out into the community about the school. (In a sense I think the biggest thing we did to improve the community/school relationship was to improve program and programming, so that students were happier and more successful in school.) A bilingual newsletter, called the 'Good News,' was published monthly and focused on good things happening in the school. A show on community radio featured students reading from some of the work they had written.

Several strategies were developed to bring parents into school – assemblies, talent shows, open houses, and science fairs. As the theme planning progressed and as more 'Inuit perspective' came into the program, specific elders were brought into the school. Rather than hire one individual to tell stories or work with students, different elders were invited into the school for each theme to share an Inuit perspective with the children. During some themes, when elders could not easily come to school, the students had an open-line show at the radio station that invited elders to phone from their homes and share stories. During the 1990/91 year, the assistant principal and another Inuit teacher from the school helped form meetings of mothers and of fathers to talk about the difficulties involved in raising children and teenagers. In a community sadly lacking in support services, where there have been eight suicides of youth between fifteen and thirty years old from 1983 to 1991 (LeChat 1991), such a service is incredibly valuable.[28]

Generally, the whole philosophy of 'catching 'em being good' and more solid programming brought more parents to the school. Children were doing much better in school. They were being more successful in math and in reading and writing. There were fewer discipline problems.

Children were noticed for their achievements, so parents were more inclined to want to visit the school to hear about those achievements. More parents came to parent/teacher interviews in the third and fourth year and they began to drop in more often at assemblies, science fairs, and social nights. I think that, generally, parents began to see the school as a place that cared about their children. The school breakfast program became a visible manifestation of that caring.

School Breakfast Program

In the book *Reading, Writing and Caring*, the authors remind us of the importance of Maslow's hierarchy and talk about the fact that teachers can't teach a child academic skills until the more basic needs of food, shelter, and security are met (Cochrane et al., 1984).[29] I understood this intellectually at the time I went to Anurapaktuq, but I think it was becoming involved in the breakfast program that really helped me to internalize what 'meeting the kids where they are at' really meant.

Many of our children came to school hungry. In a student survey that we conducted for Nutrition Month in 1988, we found that over 50 per cent of the children had not eaten anything before coming to school. In most Inuit homes breakfast does not happen the way it does in TV commercials. Often it is the child's responsibility to get him- or herself up in the morning and off to school. Food may or may not be available. Given the high rates of unemployment and extreme overcrowding in the community, there were many homes where food was not available for many days in a row at certain times of the month. More than one parent told me on several occasions that they would not wake the children up for school because they would wake up hungry since there was no food in the house. When possible, extended family would try to help families in need, but the harsh reality was that, for many families, times are getting harder and harder.

A teacher in the primary grades first talked about the possibility of creating a breakfast program, and we brought the idea to the rest of the staff. To our surprise it was met with mixed reaction. In the 1960s the government used to provide a hot breakfast program in most schools in the North. The program was viewed by some staff members as taking responsibility away from the parents and was thought to be paternalistic – reverting back to a colonial practice. Some staff argued that it was the parents' job to feed kids and if the school started doing it parents would never learn. The hot breakfast program was cut in the early 1970s – probably more because of budget cuts than on any ideological grounds.

In my first year as principal, I think that I was still too concerned about everything having to 'come from the staff.' I misinterpreted my role as leader and felt I couldn't or shouldn't go against the majority. My husband, who had worked on breakfast programs in the States in the 1960s, helped me to see that my job was to help lead people to the best decision possible, and that sometimes, perhaps frequently, the best decision possible is not the view of the majority. He also helped me to see that, although we might like to think that feeding kids is the parents' job, if it isn't happening it is the children who will suffer.[30] Children who have poor nutrition do badly in school and are likely to drop out and repeat the cycle of poverty that their family was trapped in. He also told me of research in Boston (Meyers et al. 1989) which indicates that the single most effective and the cheapest educational intervention to help disadvantaged children have success in school is to feed them a good meal once a day.

Armed with that information, with renewed courage, and with verbal support from the Community Education Council, but with no money, we set off to set up a breakfast program. Luckily, the community health nurse was able to help, and in March 1988, during Nutrition Month, we got together enough money and donations from local and regional businesses to offer hot chocolate, crackers, and peanut butter to our students. We kept track of how many children were eating this meagre 'breakfast'; on any given day over 90 per cent would want this snack. We kept rough data on how the children and the teachers felt about the program, and after the first month we all agreed that this was a worthwhile activity. The logistics left something to be desired, as we were in the old school and there was only a small kitchen and no washing facilities in each class. But this pilot breakfast program flew, and all staff became convinced of its merit.

We limped along the rest of that school year with any food we could beg or borrow, and received some private donations from individuals. The second and third year of the breakfast program we wrote to private foundations and were able to secure enough funds to keep it going. The food we supplied was certainly not enough to meet the real nutrition needs of our students, but it did help them to start their day with a little something in their stomachs. Our effort also communicated a strong message about caring to the students. Each day at 9:00 a monitor from each class went and picked up the food prepared by staff. Back in class someone handed out the food, and children sat and talked and did morning discussion while eating.

One member of the Community Education Council praised the breakfast program and said that when he was an orphan, he appreciated the kindness of people who gave him food when he was hungry. Perhaps, through the breakfast program, our students could come to understand that school is really a place for reading, writing, and caring!

Assessment

Cummins states that assessment strategies for minority children often do not work in their favour and in fact may even penalize them (Cummins 1986).[31] When I arrived in Anurapaktuq it was difficult to know 'where students were at' because of the frequent teacher turnover and the lack of clarity that existed around evaluation and assessment. Most, if not all, assessment was done in English, with little understanding of how to account for the second-language learner. I think it would be safe to say that we didn't have a very good idea of how most of the students were functioning academically. This was reflected in the lack of clarity on promotion in the school. It seemed to me that, as a group of educators in 1987, we knew very little about the students we were working with.

The realization that traditional assessment or evaluation tools had, for the most part, not been helpful to us enabled us to take a fresh look at assessment. We also benefited from being in the school at a time when much new information was emerging from the movement to mainstream special-education children and from the whole-language movement on different forms of assessment.

I have often heard other principals be hesitant about theming and teaming because they want to know how progress will be charted, how teachers will know what's been covered, how material will be stored, how students will be assessed and evaluated. Frankly, I don't think that you can address those issues in the beginning. I think you have to start at the beginning – or 'go as far as you can see and when you get there you'll be able to see farther.' Geela taught us about that. If you're going to do something that is different and innovative, you can't do it all at once. It is only once people start planning well together, improve their instructional ability, and start kid-watching that they start really to know the functioning level of the student. I have found that only once people start doing small-group instruction in math can they really begin to talk about student progress. If you teach in a large group and only check student progress by written tests you really don't know very much about your students. Whatever kind of tracking or recording system you use will be inadequate. When you change the way you teach, and in this case when you move towards more individualized instruction, you find that tests alone may not be the best method for talking about student development. Then you move towards more varied sources of measurement such as anecdotal recording, child observations, and work samples.[32] And, of course, you can't decide how you're going to record until you have figured out what you are going to teach and how you are going to teach it.

In the beginning we were far from perfect, in fact we were still far from perfect in 1991, but we had moved a great deal in our understanding of assessment – what it is and who it is for. We came to understand that what the parents wanted to know about student performance was different from what the teachers needed to know, and so we developed different genres for both concerns. Our report card became much more anecdotal and global in nature – for teachers we kept more specific information that other teachers could use. We also learned that students needed to know about their performance – that they were often left out of the process. We established student/teacher conferences twice a year where together they would talk about performance, look over work samples, and set goals.[33]

People have argued that by doing themes teachers might not get as much material covered. I doubt that this is true, but I will be the first to say that by teaching in the isolated, disjointed, unsupported manner in which some teachers teach, little is being learned anyway. The record keeping for a class using standardized tests and large-group instruction might look neater and more efficient, but I know from the number of Baffin classrooms I have been in that most teachers in such classes don't really know the level at which each student is functioning and what their next step is. I can tell you that in Anurapaktuq, with small-group math instruction, teachers knew how students were functioning. We were still trying to find a way to record that in a systematic manner, but we were sure of 'where' our kids were. Over the four years we developed developmental-skills checklists for science, math, and health. At the end of each theme teachers would record whether or not students had mastered concepts. The booklets were not linked to grades to allow students to move at different rates through the program. The concepts of mixed grades and family grouping forced us to look at the concept of *continuous progress* – each child moving through the curriculum at his or her own rate. One criticism of theming is that students often do the same theme over and over, year after year, because teachers do not know what the previous teacher has taught. In Anurapaktuq master lists were placed in the resource room that indicated what themes had been covered each year as well as the curriculum content taught in all the major subject areas to help track topics on a school-wide basis. In the language areas we began to look at work-sample assessment and kept examples of students' reading (on tape) and writing (in writing folders); twice a year teachers would go through these samples with students. We also tried to develop systems for 'kid-watching' in classes and for keeping this anecdotal information in student files.[34] In addition, we kept track of monthly and yearly attendance to share this information with parents and students.

Our major goal was to find assessment systems that highlighted students' strengths and achievements. Finding systems that teachers could keep up with on a consistent basis and that were teacher-friendly was an on-going challenge. In my final year we began to use part of our theme-planning time to also look at assessment and be sure that students were being assessed on an on-going basis.

Putting the Puzzle Back Together

The path that we travelled from 1987 to 1991 was not an easy one, but I can say that it was a developmental process for all of us. At each step along the way we learned more and more about teaching, learning, assessment, the meaning of bilingual education, student-centredness, in fact, just about every aspect of education. It was a voyage of discovery. In retrospect it looks like there was a pattern to it all, as if all the pieces were designed to fit together, but there were times when we were not sure what our next step was going to be.[35] In the beginning we focused a lot on making language use meaningful and purposeful. At that beginning level we were talking about simply how to get our students reading and writing more in both languages. We were looking at volume – how to get more kids writing more often. Several years later, once a pattern of writing was established in the school, we were looking at the quality of writing – how to move to more sophisticated writing. In the beginning it was enough to have people set up centres in each class. Once that become routine we had to start to work on improving our system of tracking students' learning at centres and allowing them more choice there. Family grouping solves some problems of trying to treat students as if they were a homogeneous group, but it also creates real challenges in terms of knowing 'where' everyone is! So there were still plenty of challenges for us, for me, in 1991 at the school. We were far from cruising on automatic pilot. Our challenges became different from those of a school that was just starting out on the journey. What lay ahead was the challenge to create a school that would allow children to be cared for and respected, and encouraged to become self-directed learners.

Trying to describe the process of program evolution in Anurapaktuq is somewhat difficult because it did not progress in a straight, linear fashion. Program is also intricately intertwined with issues of staff development and assignment which are discussed in the next chapter. However, to summarize this chapter, I would stress the important step forward we all took when we decided that programming and program were things to be shared among all the staff – that no one person had to, or probably could, do it alone. Theming allowed us a forum to look critically at how the program was put together and an opportunity to bring staff together to start teaming. Teaming occurred during each planning session: each time two or three teachers team taught in math, each time people had to share a space for an expressive-arts group, each time people worked together to make centres for each other. Teaming helped people to come out of their classrooms and see the bigger picture of the school program and their responsibility to help contribute to the total school program. People didn't, and later didn't want to, just close their doors and do their own thing in their classroom. We all began to realize that we were each other's biggest support and that it was only through working together that we could really transform this poor old school into a school where learning really did happen for everyone and where it really was fun – for students, teachers, and principals!

Notes

1 Firestone and Rosenblum (1988) describe the vicious cycle in which 'teachers who blame students for difficult classroom situations are the most likely to display "an attitude" to students, to be abrupt with them and not to explain in detail. Students receiving such treatment recognize that they are not respected which in turn reduces their commitment to the school' (18).

2 This view is further supported by both Kasten (1992) and Cummins (1986). Kasten noted significant improvements in a native Florida school that began to web the curriculum and plan schoolwide themes. As I explain later,

theme planning and preparation at Anurapaktuq actually became avenues that lead to joint work relationships and on-going teacher in-service.

3 Kasten (1992) provides a good rationale for why whole language is well suited for native communities. She feels that the major tenents of whole language (process-oriented, reading and writing parallel with oral language, teacher choice over literature, integrated language instruction, qualitative assessment, and use of inquiry) all support the manner in which learning occurs naturally in native communities. The holistic approach to learning fits into the world-view of many native people. Colbourne (1987) supports and encourages the use of whole language to teach literacy to Inuit children.

4 McLaren (1989) describes it as an important breakthrough in making schools more suited to the needs of minority students when 'we confirm and legitimate the knowledge and experiences through which students give meaning to their everyday lives' (235).

5 The professional isolation of teachers is incredibly damaging to the individual teacher and to the profession. It 'limits access to new ideas and better solutions, drives stress inward to fester and accumulate, fails to recognize and praise success and permits incompetence to exist and persist to the detriment of students, colleagues and the teachers themselves' (Fullan and Hargreaves 1991, 5).

6 Fullan and Hargreaves (1991) and Rozenholtz (1989) talk respectively about 'total' and 'moving' schools in which teachers work in a collaborative climate which recognizes that teaching is inherently difficult and that every teacher at some point needs help. Giving and receiving help comes to be understood as a means of continually improving the art and craft of teaching, not something to be feared or ashamed of, or a sign of incompetence. The first joint planning session began the process of building a supportive network around teachers in which the joys, challenges, frustrations, and hard work of teaching could be shared.

7 These planning sessions also helped to create what Fullan (1991) calls a 'shared meaning and shared vocabulary' to describe what was happening in classrooms. Teachers were able to talk about their practice in a fairly non-threatening way (although my presence as principal may have prevented people from being totally honest, as I still played an evaluative role in the school). These sessions also helped me to understand how the vision we had set for the school was being internalized by the teachers.

8 I was especially conscious of trying to model what I valued, and these planning meetings became an important forum in which to do that. I think the fact that I tried to roll up my sleeves and work with teachers on materials preparation, that I would team teach, that I would talk about

program with teachers, helped to establish the credibility I needed as a new, inexperienced principal. I also think it helped to develop trust and support among the staff. What principals actually **do** in the school speaks much louder than what they **say** about education.

9 I have come to understand the importance of theme planning in several ways. It has the overt agenda of integrating subject matter, but equally important is the forum it creates for joint work to occur. It allows a structure around which English and Inuktitut can become languages of instruction and breaks the notion of either language being a 'language program.' Theme planning allows Inuit and Qallunaaq educators to work together, to come to know each other better, and to span the cross-cultural gaps that lie between them. Theme planning further places the holistic program at the heart of the classroom, and any student with special needs can work into that program. Finally, it encourages material production at the community level, which is very important for remote, isolated communities.

10 Fullan (1991) states that 'teachers and administrators teach each other the practice of teaching' (78). I really think that by adopting/creating an atmosphere in which ambiguities and uncertainties could be expressed we could actually explore many areas that are normally guarded by teachers' professional territoriality. We could, for instance, actually admit that we weren't happy with our existing assessment scheme and could work towards developing a new one. No one had to try to save face and I found this incredibly liberating as an educator.

11 I often felt that too much of my in-service with other principals focused on evaluation and supervision of teachers with a view towards getting rid of the 1 per cent of those who are not suited to teaching rather than creating conditions in which the other 99 per cent would flourish.

12 What theme planning did was allow us to start working on creating what Fullan and Hargreaves (1991) call 'collaborative cultures ... places of hard work, of strong and common commitment and dedication, of collective responsibility, of a special sense of pride in the institution' (48). Collaborative cultures 'respect, celebrate and make allowances for the teacher as a person' (49). Essentially, just as every child had to feel valued in the school, so did every teacher. I had to realize that there were a range of behaviours that had to be noticed and reinforced. I had to rethink my notions of teachers as being totally trained when hired and had to be willing to support people who would work towards the vision. Fullan and Hargreaves say it well: the problem 'is not getting rid of the "deadwood" in teaching but rather figuring out how to create, sustain and motivate good teachers throughout their careers' (63).

13 One of the reasons that educational change often fails according to Fullan (1991) is that the innovators do not understand the multiple realities that teachers face at the classroom level. I think being at these planning sessions helped me remember what life was like for teachers.

14 Fullan and Hargreaves (1991) talk of the need to develop teacher leadership in many areas so that leadership comes from a variety of sources in the school. I think this is a key issue especially for non-Inuit principals, who are often not likely to be long-term residents in northern communities.

15 I think the importance of being present at these sessions really did allow me to understand the 'multiple realities' that Fullan (1991) speaks of. I think I had a better sense of how far and how fast we could go as a staff by being so involved in the planning aspect of programming.

16 I am continually struck by the interrelatedness of these components - theme planning helps provide a program framework, while teaming supports it and makes possible the production of more materials. Materials production is related to program goals, teaching situations, and the ability of staff members to share resources. The ability to share can be enhanced by teaming and by theme planning. These factors become highly interactive in an almost synergistic manner.

17 This approach exemplifies the idea of in-service as being on-going. Math provided an excellent medium though which many other topics (instruction, thinking skills, assessment) could be explored. Fullan (1991) says that 'teacher development and school development must go hand in hand. You cannot have one without the other' (289). The focus on raising the level of math instruction in the school furthered both program and staff issues. It was an effective way of getting at the 'second order changes' that Fullan talks about. We were changing the way that teachers interacted with students. With regard to mathematics, Burns (1989) advocates the use of small groups to teach mathematics and states that a student will learn more in a twenty-minute small-group session where there is the opportunity for the teacher to challenge the student, where the student has the opportunity to explore his or her thinking about mathematics, than will a student who sits through an hour math class where the whole class is taught as a large group.

18 Silverman (1986), in advising teachers handling students with behavioural difficulties, recommends that academic assessment be done on the student as an initial step. He believes there is an academic basis (either programming is too far above or too far below the ability of the student) for 99 per cent of students labelled as 'behaviour problems.'

19 Cummins (1986) talks about the need for educators to become advocates for pedagogical approaches that succeed in liberating students from

instructional dependence. I found that math groups and learning centres were two ways of breaking students from the need to be 'spoon fed' everything from the teachers. They became confident in exploring their own thinking, in getting on-task without the need for teacher intervention.

20 McLaren (1989) feels that the grouping of students into ability grouping is an educational practice that is unsound and unjust: 'Tracking in American schools alienates students and undermines their social aspirations and feelings of self-worth' (9). 'Schools play a major role in the legitimization of inequality' (10). 'Students in low-track are taught low status information' (10). 'One index of the persistent refusal of schools to develop a means to empower minority and disadvantaged groups is the widespread practice of tracking into ability groups. Tracking assumes that schools play a part in meritocratic selection and allocation based on ability' (9).

21 There is a considerable body of literature that supports the use of multi-age mixed-ability groupings in education: see Ridgeway and Lawton (1965), Biklen, Ferguson, and Ford (1989), Skon, Johnson, and Johnson (1973), and Cunningham, Hall, and Defee (1991). Such groupings have also been used in native communities in other parts of Canada (e.g., Kahnawake, the Mohawk territory near Montreal, Que.), as they are felt to model schools on a traditional cultural practice - that of older students helping younger ones. This is a very ambitious educational initiative, because it demands individualization of instruction and continuous progress of students. I do think it was the logical next step for our school, but I realize in retrospect that perhaps not enough time was spent with staff in order to come to a shared understanding of what the change represented in both theory and practice. Since leaving the school in 1991 I have heard from some staff members still at the school that the staff feel some concern about their ability to individualize instruction. The literature on educational change, particularly that which looks at why innovations fail in education would suggest that there was not enough time to develop the skill, practice, and theory that must accompany an educational innovation. I still feel that family grouping is an idea that has tremendous value in terms of individualizing programs for students, being culturally appropriate, and building on the caregiving strengths of the children.

22 This relates back to McLaren (1989) and Cummins (1986), who strongly argue that the problems and experience, the 'lives,' of the children must be brought into the classroom.

23 As important, if not more important, than having Inuktitut spoken by teachers in classrooms is the kind of instruction (not just the language of instruction) that is taking place. Berlak and Berlak (1981) stress the import-

ance of the interactive approach with children: 'One can only assume that children who have been schooled to expect to engage in meaningful work and act autonomously and to see knowledge as problematic rather than given, will be better prepared than those who have not, to become social critics in societies where opportunities for autonomy and meaningful work are limited and will be more likely than others to engage in socially transforming activities' (223). Given the social and economic context of the Inuit community, and the need to transform some of these aspects of the community, these are worthy goals.

24 Cummins (1990) reaffirms the use of the whole language when he talks about empowering students. Kirkness (1988) states that 'whole language legitimizes the way native people generally perceive learning. That is, learning should be based on the real world, real language must be part of it. Learning should not be fragmented; it should relate to living, in a holistic and relevant way' (88).

25 Cummins (1990) states that teachers from outside the culture can communicate a great deal of respect to students and other teachers by learning some of the aboriginal language from the children. 'Very simple gestures can dramatically boost the status of the children's language and culture within the school setting and promote increased motivation to develop both English and aboriginal language' (27). Certainly the small bit of Inuktitut the Qallunaaq spoke collectively did serve as an important gesture towards bridging the cross-cultural gap.

26 It was important for children to be able to handle language in a contextualized setting by using it to describe and analyse everyday experiences (Cummins 1990). From there students could have confidence to handle more decontextualized language concerning more unfamiliar content. Whole language builds on the child's confidence and use of the known and the familiar to venture into the more abstract and foreign.

27 As I reflect back, I see that even more work needs to be done with parents so that they understand what kinds of experiences their children should be having in school. Until there is less turn-over in northern communities there is the risk that school philosophy, direction, and goals can change radically from one year to the next. More parental understanding and involvement in education would help to maintain directions set by the school and the community. I hope we are entering a new phase in education in which parents really are seen as partners in schools and are involved more in the school. Recent initiatives by the BDBE (Parent Volunteer program, more training with Community Education Councils) have focused on highlighting the important role that parents have to play in schools.

28 I have often heard principals lament the fact that they cannot do much to improve the school until the 'community' becomes more supportive of the school. I think there is a trap in this kind of thinking. It assumes that the 'community' is somehow out there and organized and just not getting involved. 'The community' is not a static identifiable group. It is dynamic, is made up of individuals, and is organized in different ways at different times. Waiting for the 'community' to be more supportive of education before actually trying to change the school climate is like waiting for southern parents to speak in one voice in education before we value their opinions about school change. Fullan (1988) calls this 'wishful thinking' on the part of administrators. As principals we can have a great deal of influence about what happens in the school, and what happens in school can greatly influence certain parents to become more or less involved there.

29 There is growing evidence to support the important link between nutrition and literacy. A headline in the *Montreal Gazette* (27 January 1991) reads 'Study links illiteracy with hunger pangs, poor, crowded homes.'

30 Hoping the breakfast program would 'magically' happen is an example of administrators falling into 'wishful thinking.' I think we all hoped that the kids would get something to eat, but nothing was happening out there in the community to create those conditions. Fullan (1991) warns about 'if only' statements, which assume a rational model of the world. Fullan suggests that we have to turn 'if only' statements into 'if we' statements. Four years after we started children were still somehow having a small, hot breakfast every morning. 'If we' only could do lunch too!

31 Cummins found that much standardized assessment was actually racist in its structure and worked to disempower minority children. He advocated assessment based on interactions with students. Fullan and Hargreaves (1991) state that 'one vital difference is that the better schools pay attention to and try to ascertain the quality of student experience and progress using a wide variety of measures. These more effective schools also have greater collegiality, but it is particularly valued because it explicitly focuses on greater student learning' (83).

32 One new assessment technique that borrows from the world of artists is that of using portfolios with students. Graves (1993) talks about how the development of portfolio assessment has been a growth process for the people involved. He said that the vision of how portfolios could be used, and for what, has changed greatly over six years as students and teachers have come to ask more complex questions about assessment. I think that if teachers and principals would recognize the fact that evaluation is a far more complex, far more ambiguous process than many would have us believe,

evaluation and assessment could become an interesting area to support teacher development.

33 McGregor (1993) has noted that in schools in British Columbia where she worked teachers, parents and students had conferences on a regular basis and joint goals were set at these conferences. I think such a format could have exciting possibilities for northern schools.

34 Interesting and innovative ways for teachers to become better 'kid watchers' are becoming more available to teachers. Some excellent work has come out of the whole-language movement. The Center for Primary Education (1988) has produced an excellent guide for teachers by teachers.

35 I think that sometimes principals shy away from theme planning and team teaching because they are afraid it is an imperfect way of handling curriculum. They are right. It is not perfect. It takes time and energy and it's messy and sometimes it bogs down. But teaching the other way (all alone, with unrelated subjects taught in forty-minute time blocks) is far from perfect as well. Often this method looks nicer because things are more highly controlled, but in terms of student learning it is quite inferior. My point here is that theme and team planning is as much about process as it is about product. By going through the process of learning about what to teach, how to teach, what to observe, and how to record, we ended up talking about and developing our philosophies of education. That's why planning time is such valuable in-service time – you are talking about the meaning of education.

CHAPTER FIVE

Staffing

In this chapter I will deal with the important issue of staffing. A key issue to creating schools which reflect the culture of the Inuit is to have staff who reflect the culture of the community working in the school. Much of this chapter deals with issues of training and developing Inuit educators; skills training as well as empowerment are discussed. In addition, as with chapter 3, there is another stream running through the chapter that deals with issues related to teacher development generally, be it in the Baffin or in southern Canada. The relationships between Qallunaaq teachers and Inuit teachers enters here as well, and I offer my reflections on working in this cross-cultural environment. This chapter is therefore divided into five main sections. The first deals with increasing the number of Inuit educators in the school. The second section looks at teacher development. The third addresses increasing language and culture in the school, and the fourth with cross-cultural issues – being a Qallunaat administrator and teacher in an Inuit community. The fifth section discusses the creative allocation of staff.

I remember it was a beautiful day in September, the kind where the ocean is flat and everything is so quiet that you can hear the wings of the Arctic loons flap overhead as they make their way south. It was my second year in Anurapaktuq. At school we were in the middle of a great theme on rocks. The weather had been good and students were able to do all kinds of neat and fascinating things with rocks. I was running into the portable to be with a class and I bumped into Ooleepeeka on her way out the door. We greeted each other and smiled. It looked like it had been a good lesson. I was greeted by the students who immediately said to me,

'Ooleepeeka just told us that rocks are alive and Tom [their Qallunaaq teacher] told us this morning that rocks aren't living things! Who's right?' I was taken aback – one of those situations where you have to think on your feet – faced with one of those hundreds of decisions a principal makes each day. 'Well,' I said, 'I'm sure Ooleepeeka is not using the same criteria for what being alive is that Tom is using.' I looked at the list the class had generated that morning and pointed to the fact that living things move, living things have babies, etc. ... so probably Ooleepeeka wasn't thinking of that. 'Oh no,' they all chimed in, 'Ooleepeeka says rocks have babies (otherwise where would the little rocks come from) and that rocks move (they jump in puddles during storms and move in the ocean).'

The kids were looking at me to solve the dilemma. Who was right, because there had to be a right and a wrong here! I thought of the science-fiction story that I read as a teenager that said maybe rocks really were alive but changed so slowly over time that we as humans couldn't see it. Then I thought about how Ooleepeeka had grown up in this land, covered with rocks, all her life and she knew rocks in a way I'd never know. And here was I in this position of being the judge. Was there a way for me to accommodate both views – without feeling like I was patronizing Ooleepeeka or Tom?

I was never very happy with the way I resolved the issue. I took a raincheck and next day brought in one of those pictures from a psychology textbook where there's the image of an old lady but within the drawing there is also the image of a young lady. Sometimes you can see one but not the other, according to your perception. It was my attempt to try to show that maybe there could be two truths that exist at the same time.[1] This incident stands out in my mind because it showed me in a dramatic way how different my perspective and the perspective of Qallunaaq can be from that of Inuit, and how the knowledge that Inuit have of the land, of life, of the world sometimes intersects with the knowledge that Qallunaaq have of those same realities; but sometimes doesn't. This example illustrates clearly where the two knowledge bases did not intersect. This incident was one of many that helped reinforce in me the fact that Inuit schools require lots of Inuit teachers teaching in them and Inuit personnel managing them, to bring across the Inuit perspective, belief, and language system and make them Inuit schools. One of the major goals I set for myself in Anurapaktuq shortly after arriving in the community was to develop and train more Inuit educators to make the school really reflect Inuit culture.

Increasing Inuit Staff in the School

One of the greatest challenges in making the schools in Nunavut truly Inuit is increasing Inuit presence in the schools. Most of the positions of power in the Baffin Divisional Board of Education are held by non-Inuit. It has long been recognized (GNWT 1982) that in order to make Inuit language and culture real and have a truly Inuit system of education, the majority of teachers and principals must be Inuit.[2]

There are many Inuit who are in training positions (previously called classroom assistants and now teacher trainees) in Baffin schools. Originally these positions were created to allow a team-teaching situation in which a fully trained southern teacher would work with a local Inuk who would be able to bring Inuit language and perspective into the classroom. It was the original intention that over the years these classroom assistants would take field-based courses sponsored by the Eastern Arctic Teacher Education Program, affiliated with McGill University, finishing with a year's residency in Iqaluit, to become certified teachers. Certainly many Inuit classroom assistants did follow this process and are now certified teachers in the Baffin Divisional Board. However, in many cases, for a variety of reasons we will examine in this chapter, many classroom assistants have stayed for years at that level and have not completed teacher certification. As such they often remain in a subordinate position within the school – both in terms of salary and benefits and of their ability to influence school programs and programming.

In addition to not having enough Inuit staff, many schools in the Baffin still experience higher than desired turnover among the Qallunaaq staff who come to teach in the Baffin. For a variety of reasons most of them do not stay long in northern communities. The turnover rate has slowed in the past eight years, but it is still not uncommon to have a school experience anywhere from 50 to 100 per cent turnover among Qallunaaq in a year. In Anurapaktuq from 1987 to 1991, the average Qallunaaq stayed only two years in the community. Such turnover can have a disastrous effect on student success and school programs. When one considers the adjustment period that a Qallunaaq teacher requires to adapt to both a different culture and the challenging teaching situation in the Baffin, if the teacher leaves after a very short time one could safely say that during their stay in the community he or she was only beginning to learn how to be an effective teacher in the North.

When I arrived in Anurapaktuq both of the issues described above greeted me. The Inuit staff members were in a minority position. There was only one certified Inuit teacher (teaching kindergarten and Grade 1) and two Inuit teacher trainees. There was one Inuk special-needs assistant to support the program for a deaf child. There was one 'language instructor' (Ooleepeeka) hired for ten hours a week to teach the Inuktitut language to older students. There were six Qallunaaq teachers, including myself; all six were new to the community. Three of those six were new to the North and two were fresh university graduates. All of the non-native teachers from the previous year had left the school – in other words, all the teachers from Grade 2 to Grade 9 were new.

Oddly enough, the solution to increasing the number of Inuit educators came from one of the greatest problems found in Nunavut communities – the chronic lack of housing. Housing for people who work for the Government of the Northwest Territories (GNWT) is provided as a benefit by the government. Housing for people who do not work for the GNWT is provided through local housing associations. A few individuals in each community have built their own private homes with the assistance of government-sponsored home-assistance programs. Outside the larger centres such as Iqaluit the above-mentioned are virtually the only sources of accommodation. There is no private market, with apartments to rent.

There is a severe lack of public and government housing in the Baffin. Communities are growing at a rapid rate and housing has not kept up with the demand. When Census Canada came to conduct the 1991 census in Anurapaktuq, thirty-nine people were found living in the first two three-bedroom houses surveyed. In many homes sons and daughters with their own sons and daughters would live in the same house as their parents. It was not uncommon for a young couple with several children to live in one bedroom in their parents' house. We had children who came to school exhausted because there was simply no available bed for them to sleep in and they could only sleep once someone else got up to go out. As well, the government has not kept up with the housing needed for its employees and so there is a severe lack of housing for teachers, social workers, and other government workers in the Baffin. In the past, some schools have been short of teachers because there was no place to house them.

Such was the case in Anurapaktuq. When I arrived the school was short one teaching position owing to a lack of teacher housing, and we had had to hire all southern couples or people willing to share housing in order to fill the rest of our staffing needs. The situation in Anurapaktuq was getting desperate with the school becoming overcrowded, and we were short teaching staff. However, that first year my supervisor from the BDBE, in an attempt to make the best of a frustrating situation, suggested that we could hire one full-time and one half-time local person (untrained) in place of a trained Qallunaaq teacher to bring our staffing up to where it should be. Without really thinking of the consequences, we jumped at the opportunity. Herein lay an important first step towards the creation of a school with a majority of Inuit staff. We had figured out a way to get more Inuit into the school, but we also had to figure out a way to train, support, and value them.[3]

Local people brought with them the enormous strength of speaking Inuktitut and sharing the culture of the children. It was up to me, with the help of the staff, to place supports around them to be sure that the programs and programming in classrooms were challenging each child.[4]

Over the four years the criteria for selecting candidates changed, and the Community Education Council and I became more clear about what we were looking for as we hired teacher trainees. Initially, we tried to choose the person who had achieved the highest grade level and who had good literacy skills in Inuktitut. The candidates did not have to be bilingual, and in fact one unilingual Inuktitut speaker was hired as a trainee. (Having such a person on staff helped to increase the amount of Inuktitut spoken by bilingual staff and throughout the school.) Later we came to realize that grade level and literacy may have little to do with how a person relates to children. As time went on, we tried to hire candidates who demonstrated above all an interest in children and good interpersonal skills. We figured that if they had a good sense of themselves as people we could work on upgrading their skill levels.[5] In a couple of instances we hired people who seemed to have good interpersonal skills but were very weak in their writing skills in Inuktitut. However, through the process of reading and writing daily with the children, the literacy skills of these trainees improved very quickly.

In bringing local people in we improved the school in several important ways. The first was that of strengthening Inuit language, culture, and identity in the school. The more Inuit staff we had teaching in Inuktitut, the more *real* Inuktitut became and the more the Inuit perspective and belief system was present. We could move Qallunaaq teachers up in the school and make the primary end function totally in Inuktitut. We could bring Inuit staff up into the senior end and have them work with Qallunaaq teachers so that senior students could get more instruction in Inuktitut. We could move our good primary teachers (Inuit and Qallunaaq) into the junior-high area and make that more child-centred. The more Inuit were working in the school, the more that Inuit culture and beliefs would be present in the school. It is almost impossible to say you are running an Inuit school system when the majority of the teaching staff comes from elsewhere and does not speak the local language or understand its culture.[6]

Second, by having local people involved in the school, the problem of high staff turnover could begin to be addressed. The more we can involve and train local people, the more likely they are to stay in the community or in the Baffin, and this should create more stable programming in our schools.

Throughout the four years we began to use every opportunity to employ local Inuit in the schools. There had almost been an unwritten rule that if you had a government house you had to put a teaching couple in that house because of the housing shortage. Many times schools do not get the exact educational match they would like when they hire a teaching couple. Often one member suits the school's needs and the other is less than a perfect match. In Anurapaktuq we started looking at hiring the teacher that best fit our needs. If that happened to be a single teacher, we would hire that person and then hire untrained local teacher trainees and place them in the classroom under the direct supervision of a trained teacher. Through this process we were able to arrive at a situation in 1991 where ten of the fourteen staff members were Inuit educators.

Having this many Inuit staff was instrumental in creating the cultural base and relative staff stability that we achieved in the school during the four-year period. However, certain adjustments had to be made to accommodate bringing so many untrained people onto the staff.

Teacher Development

By bringing untrained people on staff and placing trainees in classes without a full-time Qallunaaq teacher present at all times, we needed to be sure that adequate support and training was being provided to these trainees. It is here where issues of programming and staff development are intertwined. By theme planning as a group several experienced teachers were able to provide immediate support to these teacher trainees. Divisions (Primary K–3, Intermediate 4–6, and Junior 7–9) met biweekly to plan their theme plan in detail. *At the end of each day teacher trainees met with their trainers to debrief and plan for the next day. Because several classes were doing the same theme, I, as a teacher trainer, could meet with the primary planning group each day and plan for an hour or so after school.* Teacher trainees were provided with modelling and support in the class each day during supported math and writing groups. Through this 'team' support, experienced staff members were continually helping trainees with ideas for lessons, with classroom management tips, and with materials production.

The reader may get the impression that it was only teacher trainees who required training, development, and service. I learned very quickly from being in classrooms that all of the staff felt they needed support – in new areas of curriculum such as whole language, in the writing process, in hands-on math, and in areas of management and assessment. The mechanisms that were developed and are discussed here benefited all staff members.

The short after-school meetings each day were a chance to see if any problems were developing in classes. I would sit in on these meetings each day.

But theme-planning and after-school meetings did not bring the whole staff together – usually primary and junior/intermediate groups met separately. I felt we needed a forum in which the whole group could meet. For example, one of the goals for our first year involved making language meaningful in the school – both languages. Luckily, this was just at the time that 'whole language' was becoming popular, and many staff members were interested in learning more about this. We needed to have a time when we could work at building up our skills, and so we began to use Thursday lunch hours as a formalized vehicle for improving our skills.[7]

The process of developing a structure to address professional development needs began in October as the 'early easy phase' was just ending. This is a phase that teachers new to a community or to the North often experience. Most Qallunaaq teachers come with a genuine wish to make a contribution to the North, and indeed they have and probably will continue to have a role to play in supporting northern education. Unfortunately, because most formal teacher training takes place outside the classroom and poorly prepares people to work with children, most teachers lack the skills and support necessary to deliver a program that really meets the child's needs. During August and September the children are usually excited about being back at school and are excited about the new teacher. Often the teacher's personality and excitement is enough to sustain the child and there are usually few discipline problems. The weather is nice, the kids are happy, and the teacher feels like it will be a good year. Round about October, as the sea ice starts forming and the daylight starts creeping away and the charm of the new teacher is wearing off, the teacher (unless supported) starts to have difficulties figuring out how to get the kids to work in groups or how to accommodate the different skill levels in the class.

New Qallunaaq teachers often fall into committing one of two common mistakes related to second language. The first is that the teacher judges the student's language ability in English by his or her *conversational ability* (which is usually quite good), makes no allowance for the fact that he or she is teaching second-language students, and aims 'too high' (covers material too quickly), so that students become frustrated. Or, secondly, the teacher looks at the student's written English or reading ability and assumes the student is far below the grade that he or she is teaching. In other words, the teacher judges the students' cognitive ability by the level of their written English.

You'll often hear new teachers say that they teach Grade 7, but that their students are really at a 'Grade 2 level.' The teachers water everything down so much that the students become bored. When teachers aim their work too high or too low for the students, the students start to react in a normal and predictable fashion: they start to misbehave. Teachers begin to panic about this misbehaviour and will try whatever strategies are available to them. Usually, in the absence of support in planning and instruction from other teachers, teachers will start to become more and more punitive and resentful of these children who do not appreciate the fact that this Qallunaaq has come north to teach them. I have seen this happen time and time again. Those same teachers who, in August, talked about child-centred learning and creating a positive, nurturing environment where every child can learn sometimes become the ones wanting the school to become tougher in its discipline, and to start expelling children. They often revert to a very controlled but ineffective teaching style. These teachers are often disappointing themselves and the children with whom they work.

It was October of my first year in Anurapaktuq and some of this was happening in our school. Although we had agreed that we would focus on the good things happening in the school and reinforce all that reading, writing, hard work, and cooperating, the students began testing the limits. Also overall programming was still weak, as we had not begun theming and teaming yet and programs were not meeting the students' needs. It was before we had really started small-group instruction, supported writing groups, or expressive arts. We were just getting our feet wet as a staff.

In an attempt to in-service the staff on behaviour management, I suggested that as a group we work through a video series that dealt with issues of classroom management. We began to meet Thursdays at noon hour and we went through this series. Some people brought a lunch and I started by bringing soup or something simple to share as we worked. Later staff took turns preparing food for others. Teachers who were mothers could keep their children at school and food was also provided for the children.

These in-services provided us with a time when we could get together, without the fatigue that comes at the end of the day, and talk constructively and with great focus about programming. These sessions turned into our weekly in-service forum.[8]

The Thursday in-service turned out to be an important part of the staff-development process, on many different levels. First, it allowed us time to constantly in-service ourselves and each other. It kept us updated and fresh, and provided a chance to 'teach' new skills to each other. We started with behaviour management, but over the four years we worked on a wide range of topics – the writing process, publishing, manipulative math ideas, suicide, cooperative learning, dealing with abuse, art ideas, and sharing Inuktitut songs, to name a few. Initially, I led the majority of the workshops, but over time staff members became involved and worked to lead these sessions. Sometimes it would become apparent in our planning meetings that an area needed support – for example, many teachers might be finding similar difficulties coming up with art or math ideas. The BDBE and Department of Education were often sending new materials or teaching suggestions that needed to be shared with staff. Any visiting consultant or superintendent was asked to lead one of these sessions when they came to visit. The sessions created a sense that we were all still learning and still discovering new things in education.

As a principal I think the fact that I was a learner along with the teachers helped to communicate the fact that I believed we were all in this together. In a way the sessions helped bridge the gap between practice and theory. Too often, especially in isolated communities, teachers only get to reflect on their teaching when they go away to a conference or take a course. Usually they are too busy with the act of teaching to have time to think about it or share ideas about it. In these Thursday in-services we actually got to talk about educational issues.[9]

As a principal I found these in-services to be very important in taking a proactive stance with staff. Because I was in classes so much I could see the needs of the whole school. I could see when work was needed with one teacher or when several teachers were expressing the same needs. If there were several teachers having difficulty with a certain subject area then we could organize in-service around this need. One of the topics that we highlighted early on was writing and publishing, since we all wanted more information on the writing process.

A second and important function of these Thursday in-services was to help create the sense of team that we needed to have in order to make the kind of programming developed possible. Gradually, staff began to work in pairs to prepare food for the in-service and to present workshops to the group.[10] Staff who might not normally have the opportunity to work together (primary/senior, Inuk/Qallunaaq) could work together, and as they did they began to come to know one another in an important way. We also did specific activities to help build that team feeling – from having a weekly guessing game on who had done what on the staff, to all learning songs from the Inuktitut song book that we could sing at assemblies, to cooperative activities that focus on team building.

As a principal you cannot influence people unless you have access to them. These Thursday in-services provided an important forum for reinforcing the direction we had set as a staff and, where necessary, providing training to get there. Very early on we had eliminated the 'staff meeting' – which I consider to be a huge waste of educators' time. We provided different ways of handling material that is usually covered in a staff meeting. Much of what goes on at such meetings is one-way information from the principal to the teachers, with no discussion intended. In our school this information was handled through a staff information sheet given to staff each Monday morning with a list of upcoming events of the week, news from the board office, and some note of encouragement, along with a quotation of the week. Thursday in-services were spent on some sort of professional-development activity. Ideas for these sessions came from needs expressed at planning sessions or by teachers as I worked with them in classes.

If issues arose that needed staff discussion, then we tried to handle that through the school team. The school team was a small, workable group that met to discuss individual, class, or school needs and develop a strategy to solve problems. Initially, a teacher who was working with a student with special needs would present to the school team information about the student and any challenges that the teacher was having with the student. The team, chaired by the principal, would brainstorm solutions for the teacher and the program-support teacher would follow up with the teacher in developing the child's program. The school team was originally intended to be a forum for planning and programming for special needs in the school,[11] but as we moved towards theme and team planning we were doing much of the troubleshooting at the planning level and so did not need to bring individual student's problems to the team. The team, which was used for larger school-wide issues, was a very focused group that met as needed. It discussed a problem at length and suggested solutions. Members brought their solutions back to the staff, but there was not an open staff meeting to discuss solutions. If staff members were interested in having input, they had to do so at a specific team meeting and not use time scheduled for in-service. I think this set-up worked successfully and communicated an important message to staff: 'We think your time is valuable and should be spent working on programs and with kids. We won't waste your time sitting through staff meetings.'

As a principal I found that this system worked well. It forced me to be organized each Monday and get the information bulletin out to staff. I was able to set up the Thursday in-service as an important time to build team spirit and also work towards improving instructional skills. It was also of great reassurance for me to know that the school team was a problem-solving group that was available to me when we needed to discuss bigger issues.

Another area of teacher development that was very important at the school was trying to bring out the leadership potential in each staff member.[12] I simply couldn't do all the instructional training at the school – I often lacked the necessary language, skills, and time. Because I was in classes so much I was able to see the enormous talent we had on staff. Very early in my principalship I encouraged teachers to lead staff in-services and workshops. I encouraged staff, particularly Inuit staff, to move out of primary and into the 'big' classes, assuring them that they had the skills to work with older students. I encouraged teachers to team teach, to teach children older and younger than they were used to. I actively encouraged teachers to take courses, to present at workshops, to visit other schools, and to work with other teachers. For all of them I believe it was a big risk. Moving from what you know and are familiar with to what you don't know is a risk, but I think I worked hard to develop teacher trust in me so that they were willing to take risks. One of my greatest rewards as principal was to see teachers developing increasing skills and confidence as we worked together. As our confidence grew, so did our sense that together, at the community level, we could meet most of our personal and collective needs.

Increasing Inuit Language and Culture in the School

Inuit educators gradually became the mainstay of the teaching force in Anurapaktuq, but not overnight. In the interim, even with the minority of the staff being Inuit, we worked on ways of increasing the presence of Inuktitut and Inuit culture in the school. From talking to some of the older students in other communities I had learned that there was often a perception that the Inuit staff did not teach very important things. They almost always worked with very young students. (It is not unlike the gender bias that many women teachers faced when primary was only taught by women.) Or students in older grades saw that the Inuktitut language program consisted mostly of puzzles and word searches. The really important 'stuff' like math and science and junior high was taught in English and by Qallunaaq!

One of our first tasks as a staff was to try to raise the profile, and increase the presence, of Inuktitut language and Inuit culture and identity throughout the school. It is in this area that the program and staffing issues become tightly intertwined.

One of the first and probably 'simplest' ways of working towards increasing the presence of Inuit culture in the school is by the use of themes, as described in chapter 3. For example, by having the primary staff do theme and team planning together it meant that at the primary end there was a majority of Inuit educators. Had each class planned alone, you would have had a situation where one confident Qallunaaq teacher is planning (in English) with one, usually less confident, Inuk teacher trainee. What often results is a strong trend towards English programming from a Qallunaaq perspective. In the larger context of team planning, however, the Inuit teacher and teacher trainees often discussed the program from an Inuit perspective and in Inuktitut. My presence and that of other Qallunaaq at these meetings sometimes made discussion more awkward, since people were conscious of us being excluded, but gradually over four years we were able to have more and more Inuktitut discussion at meetings. This fact alone helped to raise the profile of Inuktitut, which over time, started to become a language that adults could use to talk about really important things like planning program. Over the four years, primary planning sessions were conducted more and more in Inuktitut.

In the older classes the use of theming and teaming also helped Ooleepeeka, the 'language teacher,' in her work with the older students. Even though, at the beginning, most of the program for Grades 4 to 9 was still taught in English by Qallunaaq teachers, at least Ooleepeeka could start to develop a language program around a topic rather than trying to deal with language in the abstract. Students began to see that it was possible to talk about the sun, moon, and stars, not just in 'Science' but with Ooleepeeka as well. Eventually, as we increased the presence of Inuit staff in the senior end of the school by increasing class sizes and reassigning teacher trainees, we were able to increase the instruction time in Inuktitut so that by 1991 students in Grade 9 were spending as much as 40 per cent of their day in Inuktitut, with topics from health, social studies, and even science being taught in Inuktitut.

There were other strategies that helped us to enhance language and culture. In my second year I encouraged Qallunaaq teachers to move out of the primary classes and put teacher trainees in classrooms where, rather than sharing with a Qallunaaq teacher, they did much of the classroom instruction in Inuktitut. Since we had the support of theme and daily planning and of team teaching, I was confident that these trainees could take charge of these classes. This led to much more instruction in Inuktitut in the primary end.

The whole-language movement provided us with other strategies to help make language come alive. The publishing program at the BDBE allowed us to have books available in Inuktitut in classes, and we began a 'take a book home' program in which children took books home to read. As a staff we worked our way through the writing process, and children began doing much more writing in both their first and second language.

On a symbolic level we tried to make sure Inuktitut was visible throughout the school. Lots of student writing was displayed; the hallways were labelled and covered with print so children had lots to read. The telephone was answered in Inuktitut by all staff members. Qallunaaq staff tried to greet parents and students in Inuktitut.[13] Inuit staff were encouraged to use Inuktitut among themselves as much as possible in the staff room, and in the hallways to model for children.

Cross-Cultural Issues

If the challenge of my work with the Inuit trainees was in the area of skill development (how to be a teacher), I would have to say that the challenge of my work with Qallunaaq teachers involved attitude development. Helping Qallunaaq learn to be effective teachers of Inuit students is an important task for principals. I know that as a new teacher in Pangnirtung I committed many cultural gaffes and was often totally unaware of the gaffe committed! One of my most obvious was deciding to do a unit on flies and maggots with a Grade 4 class. Most Inuit students have a fear of, and repulsion towards flies, so this theme took off like a lead balloon. There were many times, in Pangnirtung and beyond when I was inappropriate in my way of interacting with students, of disciplining them, and of dealing with parents. I was exceptionally lucky to have worked for two years with a very good teacher trainee, and from watching her I think I learned some about what was appropriate and not appropriate. It is not so easy for teachers who come to the North and do not have the privilege of working with an Inuk in the classroom. They are often left on their own to try to wade through the cross-cultural maze.

A fellow principal once told me that as a Qallunaaq the more experience I had with both poverty and isolation the more I would understand the North, because much of what I would see around me was greatly affected by those two factors. It was therefore very difficult for new teachers who came from middle-class, white, southern urban experiences – virtually all of us – to have any means to analyse life in the village.[14] Often teachers took stereotypes about native and poor people with them, and brought them into their work. I remember one teacher who had taught in another native community in another part of Canada. I think she found the experience to be quite frightening, and felt that things would be more peaceful in the Baffin. However, she took those previous fearful perceptions with her. One day, only several weeks after her arrival, she came to school carrying a plastic gun and a stick that had been left at her front doorstep. She handed them to me with a scared expression on her face and told me that some older students had left them there as a sign they were going to knock her out (with the stick) and kill her (with the gun). I thought a child had left his toys on her step, but she read the situation in a completely different way. In fact, her perception of the community became quite tainted by this experience. She was often tense. I think people then sensed her tenseness and were stand-offish. This reinforced her perception that people hated her and this attitude, this discomfort, came right through into her teaching. I tried through our in-service, through planning, through discussion, through orientation with the new staff, to help her to read her situation a different way. One day almost two years later, as we were trying to look at program modifications for a child who was acting out in class, she looked up at me and said, 'Why do these kids need so much? I didn't have any of this stuff when I went to school!' Then and there I realized that, in spite of the energy and time I had spent trying to support this teacher, I had not changed or broadened her outlook in any way. She still did not understand that, relative to almost every child in our school, she had come from immense unearned privilege.

I arranged orientation sessions for Qallunaaq teachers to talk about issues related to working in a cross-cultural situation. I also tried to use every occasion to have Qallunaaq and Inuit work together to plan and to share experiences so that both groups would start to see each other as partners.[15] Our Thursday in-services were often a forum for building team and for learning some Inuktitut. In addition, home visits helped Qallunaaq to enter a bit into the children's world.

For almost all of the Qallunaaq it was their first time working in a cross-cultural situation where they were the minority. It was interesting to watch how people varied in their responses. Those teachers who seemed to have a good sense of themselves were able to reach out, to ask questions, to check out situations, and to start to explore the community and the culture and find its differences and richness. These teachers found teaching and living in the community rewarding and contributed to the school's success. Others, like the teacher I described, were not able to venture outside themselves, were always fearful, and stayed within the white world.[16] They rarely partook of community events, they fraternized almost exclusively with other Qallunaaq, and they were critical of the parents and community. They often resented other Qallunaaq who would not socialize outside school with them with the accusation of having 'gone native.' On a couple of occasions it made for some very tense moments on staff.

Qallunaaq who understood the school's goal of enhancing Inuit language, culture, and perspective in the school were able to adjust to the increased use of Inuktitut throughout the school. They could be in a room where two Inuit were speaking Inuktitut and understand that this was perfectly normal and natural if the conversation did not pertain to them and that they were not being 'excluded.' Qallunaaq who did not understand the school's goals sometimes felt excluded and even paranoid. One member told me that he thought everyone in the staff room was talking about him.

Trying to understand the Inuit world without understanding Inuktitut is indeed a challenge. I always felt that I was only beginning to learn about the Inuit world. I used the experience and expertise of the Inuit on staff and also of Father, the local priest who had lived almost half a century in the North and spoke fluent Inuktitut, who helped me understand the historical and social perspective. A source of disappointment and frustration for me as a principal was the struggle to help other Qallunaaq develop greater cross-cultural understanding. If a teacher lacked skills I usually could help them gain the skill. If he or she didn't know how to teach long division I could show them that. But when a teacher had an underlying 'bad attitude' about the children that he or she was working with I had a much harder time knowing how to bring that attitude to the surface and examine it. I suppose I tried to put people in as many positive situations as possible with Inuit, but basically their attitude clouded their view, preventing them from seeing what was in front of them. Many Qallunaaq educators feel that cross-cultural understanding involves learning more about Inuit people. I feel that our first step as Qallunaaq is to examine the cultural values and beliefs we bring as non-native people.

As an administrator in a school where an increasing number of staff members were Inuit I had to re-examine my values about school and education. If the school was to be staffed by Inuit and run exactly like a school in Dartmouth, Nova Scotia, would that be a good thing? Certainly the more new cultural attitudes, values, and practices were being brought into the school, the more the school should be transformed.[17] This is an area that I needed to work on continually – examining my own actions as being potentially patronizing, biased, or sometimes racist. As more Inuit mothers came on staff problems around absenteeism and lateness due to babysitting occurred. I had to learn to be flexible and understand that this was a real problem for most of our staff, and I couldn't handle it just by disciplining. There were times when I felt that we should be exploring more science concepts in Inuktitut – when some of the Inuit staff didn't feel comfortable with the concept or see its relevance. Knowing when to support the problems that a staff member had and knowing when to confront those problems was always difficult for me. Inasmuch as I was asking new Qallunaaq teachers to extend themselves and try to see the world from Inuit eyes, I had to try to understand what was essential about school. Many of the rituals and routines that happen in schools no longer have meaning, but we continue to use them. I had to learn to be able to separate the essential from the superfluous. It was a never-ending exercise for me. I often wondered how another educator, perhaps an Inuk, would have responded to the children's question about whether rocks were alive or not. The longer I stayed, the less sure I was about whether rocks were or weren't alive!

Creative Staffing

One of the big breakthroughs for me as a principal was the realization that I didn't have to think in terms of one teacher = one class. As long as we think that for every nineteen students we have to have one teacher with that group all day, we are very limited, at least with the present manner in which staff is allocated. An important issue related to staffing in Anurapaktuq was that every staff member wore several hats. In addition, we knew that planning time was important to us. During our third year each staff member agreed to accept a few more students per class, and thus we were able to hire a physical-education specialist who could provide a quality physical-education program and allow people planning time and time to team teach in other classes. In my role as principal and program-support teacher I could be in the classroom, either team teaching or taking a class to free someone else to do support in another class. By creative timetabling we were able to use people in different ways and give teachers a variety of experiences in the school. During a math group you might have two adults with twenty-five children; during story time or reading one adult could supervise the whole group while a free teacher moved to support some other class. In my fourth year I would take all the primary end (about seventy-five students) to do a huge sing-song for forty-five minutes each week to allow the teachers more planning time. Once I started to see the school as a system and the staff as team players, I could create staffing arrangements to allow for such things as team teaching, theme planning, and small-group instruction.

Teachers and principals from other communities have often asked how we were able to have so many Inuit educators as part of our staff. Essentially, the process was as I have described, but I assure people that one must be willing to see that training is a huge part of the job of the principal and other staff members. I feel that we were able to provide many levels of support for these teacher trainees. Theme and team planning offered training and support through sharing teaching ideas and strategies. There was team teaching and daily planning with experienced educators to provide daily on-going support in preparing lessons. There was regular weekly in-service to address educational issues. There were Arctic College courses to train people on-site. All this took a great deal of my time and that of other teachers who were providing leadership. However, I believe it is worth mentioning here that creating change takes time and energy. We spent our time and energy building up an Inuit staff, and the effort took the time and energy of all the staff.

However, at the end of four years we had achieved a school that began to reflect Inuit culture. I know many principals and teachers who spent just as much time and energy on training Qallunaaq who would leave the community after two years. Those principals and teachers felt like they were constantly in a state of rebuilding.

Notes

1 There has been more formal recognition in the last few years of the fact that different traditional and Western knowledge bases do exist and sometimes do not overlap. The NWT Junior High Science Program (Education 1990) invites teachers to explore and examine the two knowledge bases for various science concepts. Such inclusion of traditional knowledge in the curriculum is, I think, an important sign of respect for native culture and knowledge.

2 The Baffin Divisional Board of Education's Special Committee Report on Inuit Education (BDBE 1992) recommends that by the year 2000 there be Inuit principals in all Baffin schools. This recommendation, as well as the one recommending that Inuit teachers become a majority in the education system, is supported by almost every educator in the Baffin, yet the system remains far from its goal. At the time of this writing, seven of twenty-four (30 per cent) administrators are Inuit and approximately 22 per cent of the certified teachers are Inuit. These figures fall far from the recommendations projected for the year 2000.

3 There is a wonderful book called *A Whack on the Side of the Head* (von Oech 1983) that describes examples of insight and innovation. Very often the way in which we frame problems limits the solutions we will envisage. We could not see possibilities because of our focusing on the question before us. My supervisor's suggestion, perhaps inadvertently, created a new way of looking at the problem. In a sense, within the initial 'problem' lays some of the seeds of solution for other challenges. Once the problem was reframed to ask how there could be more Inuit teachers in the schools rather than how we could find more houses for Qallunaaq teachers, the solution lay before us.

4 McAlpine and Crago (1992) refer to the fact that a minority community does have the power to transform schools. By placing more Inuit in classrooms and by providing on-site training and staff development, I think we were able to start working on 'second-order' changes in which teacher/student relationships really can be transformed.

5 To my mind the criteria for selection of teacher trainees need to be carefully considered. The formal education of many Inuit teacher trainees is very
low, and sometimes this has been used to deny them access to teacher
certification. My experience and reflection convinces me more and more
that, as with children, we must be able to take trainees 'where they are at.'
If literacy is an issue for trainees, then surely it is best addressed in the
meaningful context of a training program. The same principles of whole
language would apply. It is far too easy to use literacy as a gate to block
mature, empathetic trainees from starting real training. It should be the job
of the trainee instructors, not the trainees themselves, to address the
challenges of literacy.

6 Cummins (1990) speaks to the fact that language also has an important
spiritual dimension. He suggests that 'a strong spiritual and cultural identity
in schools may be a prerequisite for both personal and academic growth
among aboriginal students' (4). This dimension reinforces the urgent need
for more Inuit educators in schools.

7 Little (1981) states that school improvement occurs when 'teachers engage
in frequent, continuous and increasingly concrete and precise talk about
teaching practice (as distinct from teacher characteristics and failings, the
foibles and failure of students in their families and the unfortunate
demands of society on the school)' (77). Too often schools are set up like
beehives where every teacher is expected to act in a private and isolated
fashion. Research states (Fullan 1991, Lortie 1975) that teachers learn most
from other teachers, yet the very structure of schools often allows no time
for teachers to share in a professional way. And not only do teachers learn
from each other, but when they collaborate they learn about the uncertainty, the challenges, of teaching. This revelation, when shared, leads to a
feeling of shared vocabulary and shared effort (Rozenholtz 1989).

8 Where teachers do not share these uncertainties, they quickly begin to lose
self-confidence and consequently become less likely to risk any change at
all. The Thursday in-services were an important part of staff development.
They were a chance to learn, to celebrate, to clear the air, to encourage
each other through times of ambivalence and uncertainty. Given the ambitious challenges we had taken on as a school these weekly forums were a
chance to regroup, re-evaluate, and refocus. Fullan and Hargreaves (1991)
reiterate that classroom improvement will not occur until teachers begin
working in more caring and supported environments. They state that there
can be no student growth and change without teacher growth and change.
And I suspect that there can be no teacher growth and change without
principal growth and change. Fullan and Hargreaves also speak of

'collaborative cultures' in schools, which are 'found everywhere in the life of the school, in the gestures, jokes and glances that signal sympathy and understanding, in hard work and personal interest shown in corridors or outside classroom doors; in birthdays, treat days and other little ceremonial celebrations' (48).

9 The need for on-going in-service and staff development is addressed in much of the current literature on schools (Fullan 1988, Fullan and Hargreaves 1991, Berlak and Berlak 1981). Often teachers are too wrapped up in day-to-day matters to stand back and reflect on their practice. Berlak and Berlak offer a useful framework for understanding the multidimensional nature of schooling. Some of the 'dilemmas' encountered in teaching include the academic dilemma (whole child vs. child as student), the time dilemma (teacher vs. child control), and the standards dilemma (teacher centred vs. child centred). Educators are continually working through the dilemmas all at the same time. Sometimes they are conscious of some of the ideological choices they are making, but often, as Berlak and Berlak found in their study of teachers in English schools, teachers were unaware and unreflective of the choices they were making and of the impact of those choices on learning in the classroom. The authors found, however, that teachers can resolve these dilemmas by working together. They suggest that teachers need to ask three questions to become more conscious of their actions: 'What are present/alternative patterns?' 'What are the origins/consequences of the present/alternative patterns?' 'What craft/ knowledge is used/needed for present/alternative patterns?' (Berlak and Berlak 1981, 241).

10 Valentine and McIntosh (1990) look at organizations dominated by women and find an importance attached to the use of food as a means of celebration, sharing, and building support. I believe that the use of food became an important ritual and symbol of sharing on staff. Including the children of staff at these lunches also acknowledged the dual role (mother/teacher) that most staff members held. It was a 'just' gesture, but I feel it was a significant one. In Inuit society the sharing of food continues to have important social and spiritual importance.

11 The school-team model for programming for students with special needs is, I think, a sound educational model and one that is aptly designed for schools in isolated settings. For a more complete discussion of the school-team model, see Makeechak and Tompkins (1986).

12 An important element of working towards school improvement is for a principal to empower people subordinate to her or him and thereby develop more leadership among the staff. Fullan and Hargreaves (1991)

state that principals need to 'give teachers much more experience of leadership, administration and policy development earlier in their careers when they are still rooted in their classroom roles' (12). I think that one of my strengths as a principal, whether by design or out of sheer necessity, was to encourage people to step outside their classroom role and become educational leaders in the school.

13 Cummins (1990) underlines the important message that is sent to aboriginal children when non-native teachers try to learn even a few words in the aboriginal language. Certainly from 1987 to 1991 no Qallunaaq educator became fluent in Inuktitut by singing Inuktitut songs at the Thursday inservice, but this little gesture served to remind the Qallunaaqs of the energy involved in learning a second language and also to open us up a little more, in a small but not insignificant way, to the Inuit world.

14 Geoffrey York in his book *The Dispossessed* (1990) gives what I think is a good analysis of the dynamics of poverty, cultural crisis, and violence that occur in so many native communities. I think reading such a book would help many northern educators to see the 'big picture' of what is going on around them.

In addition to Qallunaaq and Inuit coming from vastly different backgrounds and experience there were challenges raised by communication differences. Not only was language a barrier in that no Qallunaaqs were fluent in Inuktitut, but even where Inuit and Qallunaaq spoke English there were differences in communication styles. Scollon and Scollon (1983) describe communication blocks that occur when bush consciousness interacts with modern consciousness in their work in a Dene community. Crago (1988) found that language use among Inuit children varied between home and school. It would be reasonable to think that differences in communication styles can lead to misunderstanding between Qallunaaq and Inuit teachers.

15 The question of how to change racist attitudes of Qallunaaq educators remains an important one for me, and it is area where I feel I need to develop more strategies and understandings. Kleinfeld (1985) suggests pairing new mainstream teachers with experienced teachers and setting up a kind of mentoring situation where experienced teachers can guide new arrivals in their cross-cultural journey. Clandinin and Connelly (1991) use teacher narratives as a way of understanding and influencing teacher practice. In the future I might explore teacher biographies and narratives with Qallunaaq to help them understand how their life story has affected their development as teachers and how those life stories compare and contrast with those of their Inuit colleagues.

16 Osbourne (1989) describes the concept of ethnic borders among Zuni and Anglo teachers. He stated that the power relationship between the two groups played an important element in maintaining borders. He found that 'borders were maintained by adults to protect their own power bases - Zunis to protect their cultural knowledge from some Anglos and Anglos to protect their privileged status as members of the dominant society' (211). This issue of borders would be interesting to explore further to perhaps better understand why some Qallunaaq adapt well to the community and others do not.

17 McAlpine and Crago (1992) present interesting examples from Algonquin, Cree, Inuit, Mohawk, and Naskapi schools in Quebec that indicate that the relationship between the majority and minority culture is dynamic. Majority culture definitely influences minority culture, but the minority community has the power to transform schools. I look forward to witnessing the school cultures that will evolve as Inuit become the mainstay of the education system in Nunavut.

CHAPTER SIX

The Role of the Principal

In this chapter I examine my role as principal and how I think I influenced change in the school. I have divided the chapter into three sections. The first looks at the philosophical orientation that I think a principal needs to have – faith, vision, and patience. The second section looks at time and how I tried to use it. The third explores the ethic of caring in relation to the role of principal.[1]

When I talk to others about my work in Anurapaktuq, I am often asked two questions. The first is 'How did you find time to do all this and not burn out or spend 75 hours a week in school.' This question is usually followed by 'Well, if you were doing all this program stuff what happened to the paper and administrative stuff that principals do?' Both are good questions, and for me a very important part of this whole monograph is trying to explain to others, especially principals, how they could set up schools and be involved in schools in such a way as to make good things happen. There is a saying 'Teachers make a difference.' It is my belief from my experience in Anurapaktuq that principals make a difference.

The Role of the Principal

One of the first things I had to define for myself when I arrived at Anurapaktuq was my role as principal. I was fortunate because at the time that I became a principal there was interesting literature coming out of the Ontario Institute for Studies in Education (OISE) on the role of principals in schools. Fullan's work on educational change (1988) very much influenced the Baffin board, and the work of Leithwood (1986) on the profile of an effective principal was adopted in the Baffin. I was able to participate in principal training during my first year at Anurapaktuq and finished my training in my second year. What was apparent to me from my own experience observing principals throughout the Baffin – from listening to teachers talk about the kinds of challenges they faced while I as program consultant and as a teachers' union representative – was that teachers needed more support to do their jobs. To be effective and help improve programs for children, principals had to take an active leadership role in their schools and become instructional leaders. They had to be willing to help create a vision about what good schools and classrooms were, and be willing to help equip people with the skills to reach that goal. For many principals this was a radical departure from how they defined themselves. Many saw their role as being the administrator – managing the school, counting the lunch money, making up the gym schedule, filling in time sheets, communicating with parents, but rarely going into classes! Most principals evaluated staff in a summative fashion and were involved only in the later stages of intervention – never at the planning end to help people with instruction.

The time I spent in numerous Baffin classrooms helped me understand the complex challenges the teachers faced and also understand that many teachers wanted help in meeting those challenges. Most teachers justifiably complained that they were unsupported and unrecognized in schools. I hoped in my role as principal to change that in our school.

Vision, Faith, and Patience

Over the four years that I was in Anurapaktuq, I realized that the three things I needed to be effective in our school were a vision, faith, and patience. I was fortunate during my time in Baffin to have been exposed to some inspirational leaders in education as part of the board's inservice: Jim Cummins, the Whole Language CEL group from Winnipeg, the Wellington County School Board with its excellent policy on mainstreaming, Wayne Holm from Rock Point, Arizona, on his work with Navajo students, and Ed Miller on 'catching 'em being good,' among others. These inspirational leaders helped me to form my ideas about education and create a vision for what our schools could be. Books by inspiring educators such as Sylvia Ashton-Warner (1963) helped affirm what I believed in. I went to Anurapaktuq believing that every kid could do well in school and that schools could be places for having fun and learning. I knew that many schools didn't realize this vision; but I understood that it was not because the vision was impossible or wrong or too idealistic, but because the kinds of structures we set up in schools often worked against, rather than for, creating these kinds of schools.

To support the vision I needed faith. I guess it was faith on many levels: faith in the vision that I believed in, that people – students, teachers, parents – really could, given the proper, caring environment, become better. The element of faith was important because there were days when students let me down, when they acted as if they didn't care, when some of them were downright miserable towards themselves and others. There were days when some of the teacher trainees, many of whom already had huge demands placed on them by their families and the community, could not let go of all their baggage and just weren't able to give anymore to anyone – especially not to the kids in their care that were so needy. There were days, after a big liquor order would arrive in town, when many parents, themselves troubled and confused, would resort to drinking binges. It was at such times that I needed to have faith in the vision that I believed in – that it was not too idealistic, that people, if supported, really could pull themselves out of difficult circumstances. There were days when all the interactions I had with people would run counter to the vision. Those days I needed faith. And that is what faith is – believing in something beyond what you see in front of you today. Believing that the caterpillar will turn into the butterfly, the seed into the flower, the non-achiever into the able and curious student.

Part of my faith came from my own family and my husband, who helped instil in me the value that people are basically good, that they want to do well instead of poorly, and want to be generous and giving rather than selfish.[2] Often the unjust and impoverished situations in which people are forced to live creates the violence and hopelessness that we see in many communities.[3] The Oblate priest in the village, Father, helped me strengthen my faith. A wise man who has been in the North for nearly fifty years living among the Inuit, Father had witnessed the many forces that have changed the lives of the Inuit. He has seen the challenges they have had to face. He has been touched by the tragedies – by the accidents, by the suicides, by the lives wasted through alcohol and drug abuse, by the confusion; and yet he still has the faith to keep working day by day to help people work to change themselves. Father often helped me to understand the 'why' behind some of the things I saw happening in the community, and he helped me to keep believing that working for change was a worthy, and indeed reachable, goal. Father often helped to provide an analysis of why certain things happened as they did. There were many issues that I did not understand. Why did caring parents resort to drinking? How did I deal with a good, competent teacher trainee who was a victim of spousal abuse? Why did the community sometimes appear to tolerate or even accept violence towards women? The literature on principalling couldn't help me with these issues. However, Father helped provide me with a historical perspective as well as a social analysis, so that I could understand why things were happening as they were. Without this reinterpretation of events by Father, I think, there were times when I would have lost the faith in people.

One of the most difficult situations I ever dealt with happened in 1990. Manniq was a bright, funny and talented Inuit woman, a mother of five who worked at the school as a teacher trainee. She had been given, in an arranged marriage, to a man from another community when she was only fifteen, and had lived a traditional life up until her mid-twenties, when she started working at a school – first in another community and later in Anurapaktuq. She had worked hard at both jobs – at being a mother and a teacher. I worked closely with Manniq in the school and grew to consider her a friend. One of my most pleasant memories of Anurapaktuq was spending a weekend travelling with Manniq and her family to another community under the beautiful spring sun. She managed to work through many courses in her teacher training program and was able to go to Iqaluit in 1989/90 to complete her final year of training and become a fully certified teacher. This final step of going to Iqaluit for a year is a difficult one for most trainees, especially for women with families. It means uprooting the family for a year, leaving behind the support of extended family and community, and going to a settlement where more challenges are present (the bar scene, drugs and alcohol, loneliness).

Things were not easy for Manniq there. Her family situation came apart and she and her husband split in a violent manner that left Manniq hospitalized. However, she managed to keep some of her children with her and continue her studies. At Christmas that year, when she came back to Anurapaktuq for a visit, she talked about how she would come back to the community as a trained teacher, occupying one of the brand-new houses being built for teachers, work in the school, and be able to take good care of her family as a single parent. She knew it would be hard, but she felt that she would be able to do it. In fact, she never did it. On February 5, 1990, Manniq killed herself in Iqaluit. My journal from that time recalls the confusion and pain that I felt around her death.

'Monday night I awoke to a phone call saying Manniq had committed suicide in Iqaluit. It was like a shock – almost unreal. We got up and cried – for us, for Manniq, for her kids and her mother. Tuesday was probably the hardest day of my life. Telling the staff, seeing her mother feeling the hurt. We cancelled in the morning – opened in the afternoon. It was a hard week – so totally unbelievable ... The graveyard was hard. Like being at a movie with no sound. The figures huddled in a circle, the sun beating through but you couldn't feel it, people crying but you couldn't help them, the rocks hitting the casket but you couldn't hear it. Little Lena trying to throw plastic flowers into the rocks ... I only started to get an idea of how bad the pain might be for them. It was such a contrast of images – the bright sun, the hurt. The beautiful land, the tragic end for Manniq. It took me all the next week to start thawing. When something would go wrong I would not even have the vision to hold up because it cracked with Manniq. The depth of healing that has to be done here. I have to have a long chat with Father to find out how he has kept a faith – a perspective on what he has done when the suffering he sees daily has been so great.'

With Manniq's death the faith did waver – I too had to go through the stages of grieving and finally come to some understanding of what sense could be made of such a senseless incident. For educators in the North, and I think especially for principals, it is important to have a support system – people who will help you have faith in the vision you see, even when it seems to crumble.

A last important thing needed in the role of principal is patience. Patience involves understanding change, the nature of change and the nature of people. Patience is understanding that people can 'only' be what they are at the moment, that change happens in small steps, that people often backslide, and that people can't change everything about themselves at once. That goes for kids, teachers, communities, principals, and school boards. Patience was involved in setting a high vision for the school and helping people to work towards it. Patience involved reinforcing people in working towards that goal but not punishing them if they couldn't reach it. Once people start to fear that they will be punished for the risks they take in reaching for a vision, they will stop moving and trust will have been broken down. Just as I was trying to help teachers become better teachers, so too were the staff and students trying to teach me how to be a better principal.[4] Teacher trainees reminded you of how clearly you have to communicate ideas – of how much you needed to model what you wanted them to do. To just talk about an activity wasn't enough. Students continually reminded me that school was as much a social experience as anything else. Teachers had to remind me that the day-to-day classroom work was exhilarating yet exhausting, and that they couldn't take on all the projects that I had in my head at once. Trainees with families reminded me that teaching is still, after all, only a job and that there are other things in life that need to be attended to other than school – from the needs of a sick child to the enjoyment of Easter celebrations down on the ice.

I couldn't expect people to run before they could walk. I might have my ideas of where the school should be, but I could only move as fast as the people around me could move. I might have wanted to have more Inuit staff in the school and have everything working well. But I had to remember that many of the trainees were working mothers who were themselves working through issues in their personal as well as professional life. If I had made the commitment that training local people was im-portant, then I also had to deal with the fact that for many women babysitting would be a problem from time to time. There was no com-munity day care, and often people ran into problems with babysitting. Some principals would say to staff that if they couldn't find a babysitter they shouldn't bother coming to work, but that means you won't have many Inuit working in your school. I had to learn to try to find solutions when teachers had to come to work with children. I had to learn what to do when staff members were working through issues in their personal lives that affected their professional lives. In the south there are alcohol and drug counselling, spousal-assault, and other support services available to people. In the small communities in the North these services are simply not available. One has a choice – to be patient and learn to support staff and work towards that vision or to simply give up and say it's impossible to work in such a system. As I wanted teachers to be patient with children, to know when to support and when to demand, to know when to comfort and when to challenge, so too I had to learn that with staff.[5] There were many times when I, in my comfortable three-bedroom house, with my supportive and loving husband, with time that was my own in the evenings, the weekends, and the summers, with no financial worries, would not be patient enough with a single mother who was teaching in the school and had not eaten for three days because she was waiting for pay day. Or not patient enough with the teacher who was scared to death to try to teach a certain concept in health or science because she really felt unsure of herself, in spite of what I thought was lots of preparation. Or with the Inuit teacher who was trying to work through her role as teacher in a community where family relationships determine how you act towards people. Or patient with students who had not slept all night because there weren't enough beds in the house. Or with students who were missing school because they had to babysit at home. Or, perhaps most of all, patient enough with myself – that I too had to go slowly and I too was allowed to fail and make mistakes and still be a good principal.

Time and Administrative Tasks

One of the biggest difficulties of defining the principalship in the manner described above is finding the time to get everything done. I'll preface this discussion by saying that, in my experience, educators in the Baffin, and perhaps in the North in general, spend more time at school than do their southern counterparts. Perhaps it is a function of the kind of challenges faced where people have to rely much more on teacher-made materials. In any case, most principals were spending as much time as I was at the job, but were not able to reap the same gains. In fact, to give an idea of how high the principal turnover was, after only three years in the job I was one of the few veteran principals in the region. I did start my day early. I am a 'morning person,' so I liked getting to school by 7:30 to have time to do my own tasks before the staff arrived. In the first year I will admit to spending far more time than I should have at school, but that first year we were building a foundation. In addition I was single, and had the time and energy to put into work.[6]

A very important staff member, a teacher from whom I learned a great deal, shared my energy and enthusiasm, and together we put many hours into the school. The fact that we were piloting so many things in the school meant that we had to develop and figure things out as we went along. Often there were no other models to follow. Later there would be a lot of the material already prepared, and other principals would be able to benefit from what we had learned. Therefore, schools that wanted to start working towards change would not have to reinvent the wheel and start from the beginning. As time went on, I also learned my job better, so of course things went easier in the second year than in the first, easier in the third than in the second, and by the fourth year I was becoming unconsciously skilled in areas in which I had been consciously unskilled in my first year!

As time went on, I also learned that there is a difference between doing the right things and doing things right. I feel that some of my colleagues who were spending as many hours as I was in school were caught up doing things right, rather than the right things. They spent hours making the reports, hours arranging files, and dealing with every problem that came their way, rather than looking at the whole picture and deciding what were the right things to be doing.

The questions of time usage and burnout need to be addressed at this point. I should say first that the hours I spent in school certainly exceeded the regular 37.5 hours. In my first year it was not uncommon for me to work several evenings and part of the weekend trying to get things organized. At the time my lifestyle and energy permitted this, and I often found the extra work exciting because it was leading us new places. Undeniably, however, such heavy work leads to fatigue and exhaustion, and I would go through periods where I would pull back. I was able to retreat into playing my guitar, outdoor activity, or reading, and found that these revitalized me. As the years progressed, and once my husband came to join me in the North, I think I achieved more of a balance between home and school, although most people would still accuse me of spending too much time in school. It is not uncommon for Baffin principals to put in time after hours, and to be honest I think I was not alone in the hours I kept – perhaps unwise, but not alone. Part of what I needed help with was avoiding the 'expanding expectations' syndrome. As we would start to achieve one objective we had set – for example, using manipulatives in math – I would start to look at what we could be doing in science. As a trainee would be mastering one skill, I would be looking ahead at his or her next challenge. I think I needed more practice at patience! Were I to do it over, I would hope that I would have a better sense of the long term – of being able to set goals and work slowly and continually at achieving them.

However, if I were to do it again, many of the structures we developed would be in place. We were making so many innovations that almost every step along the way had to be slogged out. I think of the nights spent trying to put together ideas for theme boxes. Now there are over fifty well-stacked boxes in the school. I remember writing out skills cards to be used in tracking students with other teachers. Now these are but the touch of a computer key away. I remember trying to locate and organize math resources on a Saturday and making multiple math games for learning centres. Now these exist in the math room. Initially, I had to try to plan with each teacher. As theming and teaming occurred, however, the educational leadership became shared among the staff. Initially, in-service was my responsibility; later it became a shared activity. Setting up the structures that led to school change did take time, particularly in my first and second year, and spending such time in school brought both rewards and frustrations. The fact that the programming met the needs of most children was the biggest reward of all; the frustration was that time devoted to work and labour was not always balanced with play and recreation, the very elements that revitalize.[7]

Having vision, faith, and patience are an essential part of the principal's role. But what about the administrative tasks that one associates with the principal's job. When did the paperwork get done, the meetings take place, if I was spending so much time with planning and in classrooms?

There are several answers to this question. The first is that since reading, writing, and caring were the most important things in the school, that is what I tried to spend my time noticing. By taking this proactive approach most of the crisis-management issues like dealing with disruptive students, settling fights on the playground, and dealing with irate staff, students, and parents were prevented. Because I developed systems for planning, supporting people in the classroom, and noticing the good things that happen, there simply weren't kids sitting in chairs waiting to see the principal. Thus, a lot of the administrative work that is involved with punishment and having to deal out discipline did not happen.

A second point is that there really is a myth about the amount of paperwork a principal is required to do. The essential paperwork, like the registers, the timesheets, and some reports to the main office, could be done very quickly, in about three hours a week. If a person wanted to do it well and make sure it all was neat and perfect, it would take a lot more time. My file cabinet was never wonderfully organized – it worked but it didn't have a nice system with little labels. I could have spent time doing that, but I would be saying that files are more important than people. I've been in classrooms where teachers never get centres made because they want to have every centre perfect. There is a saying that the perfect plan often gets in the way of a good plan. So with the paperwork – I got it done in the least time possible and I didn't fuss over it.

The Baffin board also made efforts to reduce the administrivia for principals. After all, if you give principals the new job of being instructional leaders, you have to take away the old tasks of administrator. In 1986 positions were created in schools by combining the old tasks of school secretary and Community Education Council secretary/treasurer (both of which were half- or quarter-time jobs). A new position of office manager was created so that this person could have almost a full-time position doing the work at school and take on a lot of the paperwork responsibilities. With a good office manager much of the paperwork could be delegated. In some school boards principals have reported that they have lost a certain degree of autonomy through such centralization, but I did not find that there was any such loss in my school.

The board office also centralized finance, so that instead of our having to keep track of finance at the community level, it was monitored through computers at the board office. This system freed up more of the principal's time, but did not take away any of the control a principal and Community Education Council had over their budgets. I felt that this was real support for principals in the field.

Effective use of the computer has also helped to reduce the time spent on paper in the schools. In my first year as principal our board had already introduced computers as tools for communication and administration. In 1987 all schools were connected up with modems to each other and to the board office in Iqaluit. An assistant principal in Cape Dorset developed a program for the Macintosh that keeps track of attendance. I used to spend about five hours at the end of each month checking every register. With the use of his program, teachers did not have to spend time trying to balance the register; I only had to spend an hour or two a month. That task could now be completely taken over by the office manager. Why spend the money they are paying me to have me punch numbers into a computer? Things like purchase orders (which have to be rewritten each year) can now be done and saved on computer, so that they need only be updated, not rewritten, each year.

The Ethic of Caring

When you ask a teacher or a principal to really care about the people they work with, you are asking a great deal. I don't think that you can talk about having patience and faith without ultimately caring about people. You have to care enough to have faith that people will succeed and patience enough to support them when they stumble or are unsure. You are asking them to touch those around them, to share their joys, but also to share their disappointments and their hurts. If teachers and principals, from their lofty positions, make decisions about how things should be without really knowing the people that these decisions affect, then they can make easy clean decisions. They don't really have to use judgment – they can just apply abstract rules, and if people can't follow the rules, then the people must be in the wrong. If everyone has to be at work at 8:30 and several mothers have a hard time doing that, well then you'd just better start looking for other mothers. If a staff member misses work because of drinking, then you'd just better dock pay and put a letter on file. When you hire a teacher, you hire someone who is fully trained, and if they show any signs of hesitancy, then they must not be very good. In principal jargon this is called making decisions from the high moral ground. They are usually much neater and cleaner decisions than those made in the 'swampy ground.'

The swampy ground is where I ended up spending a lot of my time in Anurapaktuq. I wasn't there alone, because the teachers who were really trying to meet the kids where they were at were also in the swampy ground. They were trying to tell me that it didn't make sense to assign the label 'Grade 5' to an eleven-year-old ESL student who had only attended school 50 per cent of the time in the last three years. On the high ground, perhaps, that term had meaning (although I suspect it didn't), but in the swamp it had no meaning, and a better way had to be found. Saying we would only hire Inuit teachers who were fully trained and ready to take over classrooms was a high-ground decision. Deciding to do the training and support on site with people who had limited amounts of formal training took us back down to the swamp. Working like this, I had to remember that change is possible, that positive change has to be noticed, that being fair does not mean treating everyone equally, and that rules have to be bent sometimes to suit a situation. In a sense, working like this called for a lot more judgment calls. This was a much less certain path to follow, and we certainly made mistakes as we went. Often we couldn't predict what the consequences of those mistakes would be. We literally had to go as far as we could see, and then when we got there we'd be able to see farther. We came to live by those words.

One of the important things that I learned I needed as a principal was a support network around me. If a principal is really going to care about people, then there will frequently be confusing and disappointing situations, especially in a cross-cultural setting. I found that I was providing support to the people who were providing support to the kids with challenging needs, academically and emotionally. The teachers often had each other to help support them. As principal I found that sometimes, for reasons of confidentiality, I could not turn to the staff for the support I needed. If I was having difficulty relating with a staff member or with a superior, it would be unfair to seek advice from a colleague on staff. It was important for me to have people to whom I could turn when I needed someone to listen to my frustrations, share my joys, and help me deal with my disappointments. I was lucky in the support I had from my husband, from Father, from fellow principals, and from people at the board office. In my second year the board set up a principal's buddy system, and on a regular basis I would talk to a fellow principal in another community. These phone calls became important opportunities to provide mutual professional, and sometimes personal, support.

All too often really good teachers burn out in the North because there is simply no end to the amount you need to give.[8] The needs of the children and the communities will always be larger than the energy and caring of the people who are working in schools. That is not reason to despair, but it does mean that educators have to understand that they must find a way of saving something for themselves.[9]

Leaving the Community

I left Anurapaktuq on the same kind of day as I had arrived – a grey cold day with the winds coming off the water. I decided that after nine full years in the Baffin I needed a change of pace. I felt that I had been active and given of myself in an intense way, and I needed time to reflect, refocus, and rest. Maybe the long hours had finally gotten to me! I had several friends who had taken educational leave and had found it an important time to reflect upon the northern experience, to learn new skills, and to enjoy life at a pace that was less hectic. There was a fellow principal who used to joke that his next job after principalling would be raising mushrooms because he felt he would get visible results for the time he spent working with them. I must admit that after four intense years of dealing with issues in the swamps, issues that were never clear-cut, or that never truly ended, I did look forward to doing something that might be defined, something for which there would be a visible result at the end – like a mushroom or a monograph.

I felt that 1991 was a good year to leave the community, since the principal trainee I had worked with would be able to take over my position when I left, providing continuity in the school. It was a difficult decision for me because the school was embarking on some of its most interesting adventures. The new school building that we moved into in January 1991 was beautiful, clean, warm, and spacious and allowed a chance to further diversify program. The community had been granted a Grade 10 program. Family groupings, which had just gotten off the ground, still fascinated me as a way of individualizing instruction. Many trainees were reaching the completion of their program and were becoming increasingly skilled in the classroom. I was increasing my knowledge of the community to the degree that any outsider who barely speaks the language can. The school had built up excellent resources and materials were well organized. Thus, it was difficult to think of leaving when, together with other teachers, I had spent so many hours trying to build the school to this point. Nonetheless, it seemed that this probably would be a good time – leaving the school in a position of relative strength in a year when there would be no other staff departing.

The four years in Anurapaktuq had taught me immense lessons about life, about people, and about people's determination to make sense of the cards they had been dealt in life. The backdrop of joy and despair that Irwin (1989) describes are indeed there in Anurapaktuq. I had seen wonderful changes take place: students, teachers, community members, myself – we had all grown and changed over the four years and had come to understand that change is possible, even in places where flowers have a hard time growing. As I stood in the graveyard on the last day I thought of the number of people I knew in this graveyard: Manniq, Abina – the two-year-old daughter of a friend shot in a gun accident, Ian – a Grade 1 student who died of liver disease, Iga – who had worked at the school and died young, JP – a seven-year-old run over by the water truck, and many others who had died in my time there. I couldn't help but think that if I had worked four years in parts of 'mainstream' Nova Scotia or in Ontario or Quebec, I would never have met death in so many tragic forms, so many times. I thought of how tired I felt sometimes in this community, of the times when I couldn't give any more, of the times when I couldn't understand what was happening in the families around me. Those images were contrasted with thoughts of the spring camping trips where the white land goes on forever against blue sky, of the celebrations at Christmas where people danced and played for the entire festival, of the strength of many of the people with whom I worked daily. Anurapaktuq is like a kaleidoscope – the image of it changes depending on the perspective that I take, and for me it was important to capture these multiple images while they were still clear. Writing this story has been an attempt to create that kaleidoscope for others to look into.

Notes

1 In terms of preparation for the principalship I now realize what a wonderful training I had received as a consultant at the BDBE. Essentially, I had two years to travel to different schools, observe many teachers and principals, and notice how the principal influenced school culture. Fullan and

Hargreaves (1991) make a wonderful point when they say that 'when a school has one or two bad teachers this is usually a problem with the individual teacher. When it has many bad teachers it a problem of leadership' (87). The bird's-eye view that I had of Baffin schools confirmed me in the belief that principals do play a large part in creating the working conditions in which teachers can flourish. The formal principal training I received was far too theoretical and did not relate back to practice in schools. In reaction to this experience, when I was in a position to train a principal I used an approach that was very practical – modelling what I thought to be essential elements of the role. In retrospect, with 1998 eyes, I feel that effective principal training, like teacher training, must include elements of both theory and practice. I have found that theory without practice is just talk, and practice without an understanding of background theory easily becomes empty and hollow.

2 As I have researched this topic, I have come to understand the important role that an individual's biography plays in shaping the professional teacher. In particular, I believe my own personal narrative has shaped the principal I am. My family tradition in Cape Breton, strongly influenced by the Antigonish Movement of the 1930s, was important in forming my beliefs on the potential for change. I grew up hearing stories how 'little people' working together could tackle the big fish companies, or could create credit unions to keep money in the community. I now realize how important these stories were in laying a philosophical foundation for my work in Anurapaktuq. I now see how deeply entrenched in me is this value of downtrodden people taking charge of their lives.

3 I refer again to York (1990), who speaks of the cultural assault that aboriginal Canadians are facing, combined with the extreme crippling poverty and unemployment that has led to the manifestations we see today in abuse, violence, and despair. As a Qallunaaq I am beginning to understand the importance of working with all staff to develop a better understanding of the complex social, political, economic, and cultural forces that are at play in the community. Qallunaaq staff need to understand the many forms of racism (cultural, institutional, individual) that Inuit have been subjected to by dominant Canadian culture so that they can see the important role that school can play in combating racism.

4 As an inexperienced, young, and female principal I often felt most insecure around the issue of staff 'discipline.' Many of my colleagues would insist that we had hired teachers as trained professionals and that if they couldn't do the job it was my job to get rid of them. 'My way or the highway' was an expression I heard around the principal's table. I often wondered whether I

was being too supportive or too patient with staff because I thought it was the right thing to do or because I was avoiding conflict. Through the process of writing this monograph I have clarified for myself the conviction that if you believe people can succeed and if you create conditions in which they can do that (within limits of energy), then most of your time is spent in this supportive role. Fullan and Hargreaves (1991) state that 'the greatest problem in teaching is not how to get rid of the "deadwood" but how to create, sustain and motivate good teachers throughout their careers' (63). I feel that my style was usually appropriate and effective. I could face conflict (although it was stressful for me), but did not end up doing a lot of conflict resolution because many conflicts were prevented by proactive support to teachers.

5 Fullan and Hargreaves (1991) talk about how principals have to really know the teachers they work with and find value in the work and ability of each teacher. To me this is what we ask teachers to do with the children they teach. In a small community the reader might think that this might happen naturally. However, it is quite possible for non-native teachers and even native teachers who have themselves achieved a comfortable lifestyle to remain untouched by the lives of those around them, even in a small community. Being a Qallunaaq it was easy to forget that the way most people lived their lives in the community was profoundly different from the way I lived mine. I found that home visits, trips to the land, and community celebrations helped to situate me in the context of the community. It was time well spent, and I think it was as important and as meaningful as the work I could do inside the school.

6 Fullan and Hargreaves (1991) state that 'in the early stages of principalship, communication and demonstrating what you value is best done through behaviour and example, through what you do and who you are on a day-to-day basis' (88). Certainly in my first year on the job I put an enormous amount of time and energy into doing the above. I felt I had to because most of the staff were new to teaching or to the community. And I had a personal life that allowed me to devote that kind of time to the job. I think the effort paid off because it did set a certain tone and climate that reinforced cooperation, risk taking, and support. I now realize how close I came to overwork. In terms of replicating what happened in the school, I probably couldn't do it again that way over such a time period. Neither myself nor Jacqui (the teacher with whom I worked) would have that kind of time now. Besides, I think I have started to understand that it doesn't all have to be done today. What we accomplished was important because it did and will help other schools find their direction. I also think we demon-

strated that change was possible, but I risked throwing my life out of balance. Fullan and Hargreaves (1991) state the 'balancing the work and the life is an important protection against burnout. It also leads to more interesting teachers and more interesting teaching' (80).

7 I suppose that what I have a better sense of now, than I did in 1987, is the slow, progressive nature of change. I hope that in returning to the principalship I will have a better sense of pacing – of developing a time line along with goals and objectives so that the staff and I can see in a concrete fashion where we are heading. Certainly the birth of my daughter during the writing of this monograph has helped to pull me back from totally immersing myself in studies, and I hope she will do the same in my work life. I think I also understand better that people have to understand, experience, and be able to articulate the meaning of change. This process takes more time than I supposed, and I think in future I would spend more time 'revisiting the vision' – asking people individually to explore it and, as a group, talking about the implications of changes. In retrospect, I think I understood the change that family grouping would bring about, but I don't think I let people have enough time to work through the change themselves. I know from subsequent discussions with teachers after 1991 that the change (the innovation) was not clearly understood by all the people involved and that was probably a function of our going too fast for many people.

8 I am even more convinced, looking back now on the job, of the need for principals, particularly in isolated communities, to have a support around them. Change involves risk and, potentially, success or failure. There need to be like-minded educators who share your values at the end of a phone or a modem who can provide that dialogue, that reassurance, that feedback, that 'talking out loud' that is so necessary in understanding and implementing change. As a woman I felt intimidated and often lacking in confidence in a leadership role. Perhaps for women administrators it is even more essential to have such a support network as they work to find their leadership style.

9 In her book entitled *On Caring,* Nel Noddings (1984) talks about the real danger of caregivers burning out because they give and give and give.

Epilogue

The process of writing this monograph was a challenging one. It was difficult to use writing as a medium for describing such a complex, interwoven organism as a school. In the writing, I acted as if I could simply take a piece of the school and examine it in isolation, yet at the same time show how that piece acted in a dynamic, interactive fashion as part of the whole. However, the act of writing helped me to clarify, and also gain insight into, what I really thought and understood about each component of the school. In spite of a clumsiness, awkwardness, and frustration I felt at times towards the printed word, I also am able to see how my own understanding has benefited enormously from this process.

In this conclusion I examine the major understandings I have come to as a result of writing this monograph. One is a renewed appreciation for the intricacy of the thing we call school. On the one hand, I am awed by the involved and sometimes mysterious ways in which factors in schools interrelate and are influenced by each other. I look with renewed appreciation at the complicated meanings in the teacher/student relationship, the relationship of language and empowerment, the teaching act itself, and the role of the principal. Yet, on the other hand, I am also struck by the fact that the innovations needed to turn schools into sites where children will succeed do not entail a tremendous outlay of new money, technology, research. In a sense, I think we have a pretty clear idea of what makes for successful schools – it is well summarized, for example, in the work of Fullan (1991) and Fullan and Hargreaves (1991). The answers are profoundly simple and they relate in large part to creating schools that value people, all people – staff and students and janitors and parent volunteers. The concept of valuing people is in some ways a simple one, yet the translation of that concept into action has eluded many sincere attempts by principals, parents, and politicians.

This leads me to my second major insight, which addresses the questions 'OK, if it's so simple, can anyone do this?' and 'Why isn't it happening everywhere?' Part of what I had to fight against after 'rumours' of change and success began to leak out of the community was the charge from some educators that somehow what was happening in Anurapaktuq was idiosyncratic to Joanne Tompkins. Whatever their motivations, certain principals began to discount what was happening and argue that such change could not be replicated in other communities. I have thought long and hard about this view, because if it was and is true, it means that this monograph is nothing more than an exercise in self-aggrandizement. I think it is true that I had advantages that many other principals did not have. I had been a 'principal watcher' for two years while I toured the Baffin; I had fairly good skills in programming for students; I did have a great deal of time and energy to give to the job. Those were advantages in that I think change occurred in Anurapaktuq more quickly because of those factors, but I still contend that other principals could use the same strategies in their communities. As I stated previously, the interventions described in chapters 4 and 5 are generalizable to other communities and to other schools.

Then I return to the fact that beneath all the strategies and interventions was and is my profound belief that people can change, be productive and helpful. I think of a colleague who shared the same desire to see Inuit children succeed in schools and yet, I think, held a dim view of his fellow beings. In his interactions with staff he was often punitive and condescending, putting people down rather than building them up. Although I am certain the number of hours we put into our respective schools was equal and the desire to create change was the same, he was not able to make the teachers working with him feel good and cared for. In that sense, then, some of what I did is idiosyncratic.

To work towards change requires not only a knowledge of educational innovation but also an understanding of the change process. Part of that understanding requires having a belief system that sees alternatives and looks for growth. I could share with other principals the mechanics of how we got more Inuit teachers into the school and how we set up training support for them, but that presupposed a belief that local people were able to become the mainstay of the teaching force in the Baffin. To become involved in school change you need to have the right road map to take you where you want to go (vision, belief, faith) and you need to have the ability to drive the car (sound pedagogy, interpersonal skills). Having only one without the other will keep you from getting where you hope to go. So, to answer the question whether what is described here is just a personal testimonial, I have to say 'No.' What is described here I think can be replicated with modifications in many communities. Perhaps not in the same time span, perhaps not in the same order, perhaps not to the same degree, but positive change could be happening in every Baffin community. The principals who will lead that change must have some idea of what happens in classrooms and what constitutes good teaching. If they don't, they have to be willing to take risks and go into classrooms. They also must have a philosophy that sees the world not as it is, but as it could be. Part of principal training and in-service in the Baffin must include examining and articulating one's specific values and beliefs and seeing if a principal's philosophy supports the vision of the school board.

This leads me to another insight: the important role that our own personal story plays in how we act out our professional role. I have learned how my own story greatly shaped the beliefs I carried to the job in Anurapaktuq. I find this an encouraging, hopeful discovery, because I think that listening to the stories of other teachers and principals is important in understanding what they value and why. If we can learn that, then we can learn to either reinforce or to change those values. I see the role of stories and biographies in principal training as providing a means of reflecting with a view towards action. Casting the teacher/principal as researcher gives to the job a dimension of reflection and critical learning that we advocate as important dimensions of any learning. Research that allows teachers and principals to treat the most important work they do each day as worthy of reflection and study helps gives energy, drive, and enthusiasm to doing the job itself. During the process of working in Anurapaktuq, and during the process of writing this monograph, I felt that what I was doing was worthwhile and important work. I think that there is great potential for this kind of research to stimulate and excite many practitioners.

I think I have understood again the complex nature of change and the fact that it takes time. I believe that the change I worked towards implementing with family grouping went too far, too fast. I look back and see that training some of the trainees was a long process; in some cases it took up to five years to train someone to be competent and confident in the classroom. I often think, however, that had I given up earlier I would never have seen the rewards I saw later. I hope that I have learned to use the important continuous cycle between reflection and action. Doing things is very important, but there must be times for people to reflect on what the doing means. Too often I was swept away by the momentum of all we were doing and did not take the time to help people understand the nature of the change we were embarked upon. Perhaps it is a function of writing this monograph, perhaps it is a function of seeing my thirties slide into my forties, perhaps it is a function of having become a mother, but I think I have a better sense of being in things for the long, slow haul.

This monograph has allowed me time to reflect on cross-cultural issues and on my role as a Qallunaaq working in an Inuit community. One of the things I understand more clearly is the paramount importance of the teacher/student relationship in the classroom. I accept it as a given that quite often teachers, be they Qallunaaq or Inuit, regardless of their credentials, do not come to schools adequately trained to independently and effectively teach children. These teachers need support on a daily basis with the most basic of issues – classroom organization, teaching skills, and program – to set the stage to allow educational interactions that would truly reflect Inuit culture to occur. To put it more bluntly: just having Inuit teachers or Inuit principals will not guarantee that the desired cultural interactions will occur – support is required. Having only Qallunaaq will never be enough because of the transient nature of these educators. If we are to work towards an Inuit system of education we must be striving to have Inuit teachers in classrooms with children. Those teachers, who will best be able to understand and impart the culture of the children, must be supported to provide a program that is sound in pedagogy. Every Nunavut principal should be developing a plan for how to include more Inuit educators in the school. My hope is that Nunavut schools will achieve the goals set by the Special Committee on Inuit Education and, further, that administrators, whether Qallunaaq or Inuit, will realize the important role that they have in ensuring that the teacher/student relationship is nurturing and caring and encourages growth. I am coming to realize the universality of racism in our society and the need for all educators to try to examine and change their conscious and unconscious racist beliefs. I think most Qallunaaq need help through orientations, in-service, and contact with Inuit to examine the racist attitudes that they bring with them by virtue of being non-native, mainstream Canadians. Inuit educators too may have to examine prejudiced attitudes that they have picked up from the dominant culture.

I also realize how fortunate I was to have taken a principalship in 1987, as opposed to 1977. I see now that the bigger supports around me helped to legitimize and give direction to what I was doing. Certainly the whole-language movement provided a tremendous amount of literature for making classrooms more child-centred, more interactive. The fact that much of this same philosophy was picked up by the Department of Education in the materials they produced for the science and health program was enormously helpful. And perhaps most important, the fact that Piniaqtavut advocated classrooms where language was used in meaningful ways, where children were engaged in interactive learning, where Inuit language and culture were at the centre of the program helped me to put forward these things with more conviction in the community.

Finally, I think I have relearned through the readings, through the discussions, through the writings and rewritings of this monograph a sense of the immense privilege that it was to have worked for ten years in the Baffin. I am convinced that being an educator there is as exciting and challenging as it is anywhere in the world. It has provided me with rich experiences through which I have come to a greater understanding of myself and of people around me. That is a satisfying realization to come to at the end of this writing.

Anurapaktuq School Goals, 1987–1988

The following four panels display the specific goal statements and accompanying measures adopted in 1987/88, which were used with very few modifications throughout the period described in this work.

Anurapaktuq School Goals, 1987–1988

1. To ensure that the program offered to the students in Anurapaktuq School reflects Inuit culture and beliefs.

Measures and Strategies

- Include more land and sea trips for students.
- Show more books, films, and photos on Inuit life.
- Invite people from the community to teach styles.
- Visit, write to other communities to compare life skills.
- Visit sod houses with older people of the community.
- Include Inuit legends in program.
- Include storytelling in program.
- Include northern games in program.
- Develop respect for 'technology' – new and old.
- Use patterns from parkas, prints to decorate the school.
- Invite elders to talk on contemporary issues such as suicide, etc.
- Conduct workshops on constructing clothing, kamotiks, etc.
- Include themes that have northern relevance.
- Produce books, videos, and charts from stories told by storytellers.
- Amount of material and evidence of Inuktitut language will increase in each class.
- Parents will be encouraged to volunteer in school to help bridge home/school gap.
- PST/bilingual teacher in training/ Inuktitut instructor to plan weekly to ensure Inuit beliefs/values are part of theme.
- Include more old photgraphs of elders, traditional life in the school.

2. To increase the self-esteem of students in Anurapaktuq and to provide opportunities to work in cooperative situations.

Plan

- To encourage students to act cooperatively with each other.
- To have students receive information relating to themselves that is descriptive and outlines their strengths as well as needs.
- Teachers will acknowledge all accomplishments of the child, not just academic.
- Teachers will include a component of the health curriculum in each theme.

Measures and Strategies

- Physical education program will focus on individual as well as team sports.
- All students will buddy read.
- Students will participate in exchange groups.
- Teachers will role play benefits of cooperation.
- Students will role play conflicts and discuss ways of handling them.
- Students will work in small groups at math times and at centres.
- Students will use team meetings to solve problems.
- Older students will help teach younger students.
- Students will take turns teaching skills to others.
- A student council/spirit group will be established.
- Good behaviour will be noticed and stressed.
- Students/teachers will have interviews twice a year.
- Different forms of expression will be encouraged (art, music, writing).
- Student work will be published.
- Birthdays, special events will be published.
- A variety of different activities will be planned in which students can succeed.
- Staff will notice the positive things happening in the school.
- Students' ideas in decision-making will be accepted.
- Good News will be sent to parents twice a month.
- A Good News igloo will be set up in the hall.
- Students experiencing difficulty will be discussed at school team and an appropriate program will be developed for those students.

3. To develop and maintain strong literacy skills in Inuktitut and later in English through meaningful communication activities.

Plan

- Using a theme approach, Litening/Writing/Reading/Speaking skills will be reinforced through relevant content.

Measures and Strategies

Listening
- Use of tapes – recordings of songs, stories, directions.
- Modelling games – where students have to listen.
- Use of storytelling.
- Use debates for active listening.
- Critically listen for events in the news.

Speaking
- Interviews between teachers/ students/parents.
- Role modelling – acting.
- Choral speaking.
- Speaking on the radio.
- Tell stories of land experiences to other students.
- Public speaking at assembly.
- Chanting together.

Reading
- Book making with structured writing.
- Shared reading.
- Uninterrupted sustained silent reading.
- Read selection of story and students predict the ending.
- Reading to find info from the news.

- Have students take home books overnight and keep records of who reads what.
- Have writing up in halls, classrooms for students to read.

Writing
- Structured writing through book-making.
- Students use computers to publish work.
- Daily journal writing with teachers responding.
- Writing letters, birthday cards, thank-you notes.
- Cards for family members.
- Writing penpals or other communities by fax, inet, mail.
- Write about favourite TV show, people, sports.
- Write messages for students on the board.
- Teachers will conference with students about the process of writing.
- Writing/speaking contests in both languages.
- In-services (parent, teacher) on writing process.
- Halls, walls will be covered with writing.

4. To improve attendance at Anurapaktuq School

Plan

- To monitor and acknowledge improvements in attendance.
- To continue to educate parents and CEC members on the importance of regular attendance.

Measures and Strategies

- Use radio to remind students to go home early and remind parents it's time for bed.
- Have a 10:00 siren at the hall.
- Teachers talk about relationship between health/performance at school.
- Establish good/perfect/improved stickers and certificates.
- Make news of improved attenders.
- Prizes bimonthly for good/ perfect/improved attenders.
- Pick favourite activity for good/perfect/improved attenders.
- Ask students from Inukshuk High School to talk to school mates.
- Have parties, watch videos, dance, lip sync for rewards.
- Have students choose own reward for coming to school.
- Special trip for good/improved/ perfect attenders at the beginning of the year.
- Inform parents of child's attendance at the end of each month.
- Have CEC members and principal talk to parents of poor attenders.
- Establish a system to record calls from parents who call because their children are sick and to thank parents for calling.
- After three days' absence teachers notify office so parents can be contacted.

School Discipline Policy·

The following School Discipline Policy was developed in the first year (1987/88) of the new program at Anurapaktuq School. It specifies the steps taken to achieve the policy of 'Catching 'Em Being Good.'

School Discipline Policy, Anurapaktuq School

The School Discipline Policy of Anurapaktuq School is a preventative one. We believe that by focusing on the many good things our students are already doing, and by noticing those good things we will create a situation whereby the students will get more attention for doing the 'right' thing and therefore be less inclined to misbehave. Our ideas for this policy come from ideas from workshops by Ed Miller.

The level at which this prevention must occur is at the classroom level. The teacher is the person most important to the student and the one best able to reinforce good behaviour. Therefore good behaviour in the school starts with good behaviour in each class. The principal of this school is not the person who 'handles' discipline in this school. First of all, she is not very big and scary or frightening (as if that mattered), and secondly she is not the person best able to reinforce or punish students. The principal will do her utmost to support teachers with classroom management but will avoid becoming the person who 'handles' problems.

Therefore at the classroom level teachers are expected to:

1 Establish a few, clear, concise, positively worded rules with the students regarding their behaviour during the first week of school. These rules will be posted and referred to from time to time.

2 The teacher will establish a system for noticing good student work and behaviour. Depending on the age of the students and the style of the teacher this system will vary. It may include checklists, individual behaviour charts, group reinforcement, writing notes or daily talks with students. The system should be simple and consistent so that it will be carried out on a regular basis.

3 Teachers will write notes to students on a weekly basis and deposit them in the school mailbox.

4 Teachers will write a HappyGram about a student every two weeks – one to be put up in the school, the other to go home.

5 Teachers will contribute an article to the Good News every two weeks which spreads good news about the class to the parents.

6 Teachers will communicate in writing to students in their journal and provide reinforcement in this manner.

7 Teachers will keep good work samples to show students their progress and to gauge how much improvement a student is showing. Teachers will share these improvements with students twice a year during student/teacher interviews.

8 In older classes especially, teachers will use regular class meetings as a means of solving problems with students. These meetings will have an agenda and minutes will be kept.

9 Whenever possible teachers will attempt to ignore misbehaviour and focus on students who are doing good work in class.

10 Where ignoring is not possible teachers will develop a system for timing a student out or providing a logical consequence for misbehaviour. Teachers should look to reinforce a student who has been punished or timed out as soon as possible. Time out should last no longer than five minutes at a time.

11 Teachers should record incidents of misbehaviour in their planbooks and when repeated incidents occur the student should be discussed with the principal/PST and the school team if necessary. Parents shall be involved in a meeting with the teacher when this occurs.

12 Students will be treated in a pleasant, respectful manner by teachers. Teachers will expect students to treat them the same way that they are treated. Students will be greeted each day and be made to feel welcome. Improvement and effort will be noticed and commented on. If a student must be spoken to about behaviour it is better to do this in a one-to-one interview rather than in front of the whole group.

13 Teachers will routinely talk about the behaviour of the students in the class – not in a lecturing, nagging way after an incident has occurred but frequently when there are examples of good behaviour or when

students are having some difficulty figuring out appropriate behaviour. Role play is an effective way to help children solve problems.

14 Teachers will include the skills taken from the Health Curriculum in each theme they teach and thereby help children deal with their emotional well-being.

School-Wide Measures

On a school-wide basis many of the ideas mentioned above will be similiar.

1 One of the most positive things the staff can do to encourage good student behaviour is to emulate behaviour that they would like to see in the students. Staff will greet each other cheerfully and will work to support each other in the school. They will avoid idle gossip and professional jealousy which can taint a staff room.

2 All staff will greet students they meet in the hallway and in the community.

3 All staff will notice student behaviour and consider it their responsibility to comment on that behaviour even if they are not the classroom teacher.

4 Teachers on recess duty will try to notice good things happening on the playground. They will attempt to discourage children from tattling and rather help children look for good things.

5 If staff see a student breaking a rule, such as running in the hall, they will ask the student to recite the rule.

6 Staff will recognize achievements and successes through the Good News and during assemblies and through the school mailbox. Birthday lists will be posted so staff can celebrate these.

7 All staff will have a chance to interact with all students in the school through the student exchange program.

8 Staff will avoid spreading bad news about students in the staff room and try to keep comments about students constructive and directed in a forum of a meeting rather than being vented in the staff room.

9 On a regular basis the school team will plan special events which will foster good feeling between teachers and students.

10 If the school team decides that a behaviour plan includes the extreme measure of suspension or expulsion the school team will be sure that this action follows the guidelines set out by the school board in its guidelines and policies.

References

Ashton-Warner, S. 1963. *Teacher*. New York: Simon & Schuster.

Barone, T. 1992. 'A Narrative of Enhanced Professionalism: Education Researchers and Popular Storybooks about Schoolpeople.' *Educational Researcher* 21(8): 15–23.

BDBE. 1988. *Our Future Is Now*. Iqaluit: Baffin Divisional Board of Education.

– 1990. *Atanaarjuat School Review*. Iqaluit: Baffin Divisional Board of Education.

– 1992. *Together We Can Make a Difference*. Iqaluit: Baffin Divisional Board of Education.

Berlak, A., and H. Berlak. 1981. *Dilemmas of Schooling: Teaching and Social Change*. London: Methuen & Co.

Biklen, D., A. Ferguson, and A. Ford. 1989. 'Schooling and Disability.' In *88th Year Book of the National Society for the Study of Education*. Chicago: University of Chicago Press.

Boud, D., R. Keough, and D. Walker, eds. 1985. *Reflection: Turning Experience into Learning*. New York: Kogan Page/Nidools.

Burns, M. 1989. *Math with Manipulatives*. New Rochelle: Cuisenaire.

Carmichael, L. 1981. *McDonogh 15: Becoming a School*. New York: Avon Books.

Carr, W., and S. Kemmis. 1986. *Becoming Critical: Education, Knowledge and Action Research*. London: Falmer Press.

Casey, K. 1993. *I Answer with My Life: Life Histories of Women Teachers Working for Social Change*. New York: Routledge.

Centre for Primary Education. 1988. *The Primary Language Record*. Markham, Ont.: Pembroke Publishers.

Clandinin, D.J., and M. Connelly. 1991. 'Narrative and Story in Practice and Research.' In D. Schön, ed. *The Reflection Turn: Case Studies of Reflective Practice*. New York: Teachers' College Press.

Cochrane, O., D. Cochrane, S. Scalena, and E. Buchanan. 1984. *Reading, Writing and Caring*. Winnipeg: Whole Language Consultants Ltd.

Colbourne, E. 1987. 'Inuit Control of Education: The Baffin Experience.' Unpublished monograph. Montréal: McGill University.

Colbourne, M. 1987. 'Developing Literacy with Native Children.' Unpublished monograph. Montréal: McGill University.

Connelly, M., and D.J. Clandinin. 1988. *Teachers as Curriculum Planners: Narratives of Experience.* New York: Teachers' College Press.

Crago, M.B. 1988. 'Cultural Context in Communicative Interaction of Inuit Children.' Unpublished doctoral dissertation. Montréal: McGill University.

Crowe, K.J. 1969. *A Cultural Geography of Northern Foxe Basin, N.W.T.* Ottawa: Northern Science Research Group, Dept. of Indian Affairs and Northern Development.

Cummins, J. 1986. *Empowering Minority Students.* Sacramento, CA: California Association for Bilingualism Education.

– 1990. 'Language Development among Aboriginal Children in Northern Communities.' Paper presented at Circumpolar Education Conference, Umea, Sweden.

Cunningham, P., D. Hall, and M. Defee. 1991. 'Non-Ability Grouped, Multilevel Instruction: A Year in a First Grade Classroom.' *Reading Teacher* 44(8): 566–70.

Department of Education, Baffin Region. 1985. *Annual Report.* Iqaluit: GNWT.

Diubaldo, R. 1985. *The Government of Canada and the Inuit: 1900–1967.* Ottawa: Department of Indian Affairs and Northern Development.

Education, Department of. 1990. *Junior High Science Program.* Yellowknife: GNWT.

Elbaz, R. 1988. *The Changing Nature of the Self: A Critical Study of the Autobiographical Discourse.* Beckenham, Kent: Croom Helm.

Firestone, W., and S. Rosenblum. 1988. *The Alienation and Commitment of Students and Teachers in Urban High Schools.* Washington, DC: Rutgers University and Office of Educational Research and Improvement.

Flinn, J. 1992. 'Transmitting Traditional Values in New Schools: Elementary Education of Pulap Atoll.' *Anthropology and Education Quarterly* 23(1): 44–58.

Fullan, M. 1988. *What's Worth Fighting for in the Principalship? Strategies for Taking Charge in the Elementary School Principalship.* Toronto: Ontario Public School Teacher's Federation.

Fullan, M., and A. Hargreaves. 1991. *What's Worth Fighting for? Working Together for Change in Your School.* Toronto: Ontario Public School Teachers' Federation.

Fullan, M., with S. Steigelbauer. 1991. *The New Meaning of Educational Change.* New York: Teachers' College Press.

GNWT. 1972. *Survey of Education.* Yellowknife: GNWT.

– 1982. *Learning, Tradition and Change.* Yellowknife: GNWT.

– 1991. *Annual Report.* Yellowknife: GNWT.

Graves, D. 1993. 'Assessment in Writing.' Centre for Educational Leadership seminar. Montréal.

Guba, E. 1990. *The Paradigm Dialog.* London: Sage Publications.

Hinds, M. 1958. *School-House in the Arctic.* London: Geoffrey Bles.

Ireland, J. 1990. *K–6 Inungit, Pilot Project: Atanaarjuat School, Hall Beach.* Iqaluit: Baffin Divisional Board of Education.

Irqittuq, D. 1989. Piniaqtavut Conference. Igloolik, NWT.

Irwin, C. 1989. 'Lords of the Arctic; Wards of the State.' *Northern Perspectives – Canadian Arctic Resource Committee,* vol. 17(1).

Kasten, W. 1992. 'Bridging the Horizon: American Indian Beliefs and Whole Language Learning.' *Anthropology and Education Quarterly* 23(2): 108–19.

Kirkness, V.J. 1988. 'The Power of Language in Determining Success.' *TESL Manitoba Journal* 5(1–7).

Kleinfeld, J., G. McDairmid, S. Grubis, and W. Parrett. 1985. 'Doing Research on Effective Cross-Cultural Teaching: The Teacher Tale.' *Peabody Journal of Education* 27.

LeChat, R. 1991. Personal communication. Hall Beach, NWT.

Leithwood, K. 1986. *Improving Principal Effectiveness: The Principal Profile.* Toronto: Ontario Institute for Studies in Education.

Levy, L. 1990. *Atanaarjuat School Review.* Iqaluit: Baffin Divisional Board of Education.

Little, J.W. 1981. 'The Power of Organizational Setting.' Paper presented at School Success and Staff Development Conference. Washington, DC.

– 1990. 'The Persistence of Privacy: Autonomy and Initiative in Teachers' Professional Relations.' *Teachers College Record* 91(4): 509–36.

Lortie, D. 1975. *School Teacher: A Sociological Study.* Chicago: University of Chicago Press.

McAlpine, L. 1991. 'Narrative Pedagogy: Bridging Theory and Practice. Using Learner Narrative to Develop a Personal Notion of Practice.' Paper presented at International Society for Educational Biographies, Toronto.

McAlpine, L., and M. Crago. 1992. 'Traditional Process in Contemporary Contexts: Algonquin, Cree, Inuit, Mohawk and Naskapi Schools in Quebec.' Paper presented at Mokakit Conference, Vancouver.

McGhee, R. 1981. *Canadian Arctic Prehistory.* Toronto: Van Nostrand.

McGregor, C. 1993. Student assessment (personal correspondence). Iqaluit, NWT.

McLaren, P. 1989. *Life in Schools.* New York: Longman.

McLaughlin, D., and W. Tierney. 1993. *Naming Silenced Lives.* New York: Routledge.

Macpherson, N. 1991. *Dreams and Visions: Education in the Northwest Territories from Early Days to 1984.* Yellowknife: Department of Education.

Makeechak, L., and J. Tompkins. 1986. 'The School Team Model in the Baffin.' *Aurora*, Fall.

Meyers, A., A. Sampson, M. Weitzman, B. Rogers, and H. Kayne. 1989. 'School Breakfast Program and School Performance.' *American Journal of Diseases of Children*, 143:1234–8.

Noddings, N. 1984. *Caring: A Feminine Approach to Ethics and Moral Education*. Berkeley: University of California Press.

O'Donoghue, F. 1991 'Process towards Bilingualism in an Inuit School.' Unpublished manuscript. Toronto: OISE.

Osbourne, B. 1989. 'Insiders and Outsiders: Cultural Membership and Micropolitics of Education among the Zuni.' *Anthropology and Education Quarterly* 20(3): 196–215.

Ridgeway, L., and I. Lawton. 1965. *Family Grouping in the Infants' School.* London: Ward Lock Educational Co.

Rozenholtz, S. 1989. *Teachers' Workplace: The Social Organization of Schools*. New York: Longman.

Schön, D.A. 1983. *The Reflective Practitioner: How Professionals Think in Action*. New York: Basic Books.

Scollon, R., and S. Scollon. 1983. 'Narrative, Literacy and Face in Interethnic Communication.' In R. Freedle, ed., *Advances in Discourse Processes*. Norwood, NJ: Ablex Publishing Corp.

Silverman, H. 1986. 'Assessing Students with Behavioural Difficulties.' Teacher in-service. Iqaluit, NWT.

Skon, L., D. Johnson, and R. Johnson. 1973. 'Cooperative Peer Interaction versus Individual Competition and Individualistic Efforts: Effects on the Acquisition of Cognitive Reasoning Strategies. *Journal of Educational Psychology*, 1: 83–92.

Smith, J., and D. Smith. 1976. *Child Management: A Program for Parents and Teachers*. Champaign, IL: Research Press.

Special Committee Report on Inuit Education. 1992. *Education 2000*. Iqaluit: Baffin Divisional Board of Education.

Tompkins, J. 1991. 'Theming and Teaming in Baffin.' *Aurora*, Fall: 2–8.

Valentine, P., and G. McIntosh. 1990. 'Food for Thought: Realities of a Women-Dominated Organization.' *Alberta Journal of Educational Research* 36(4): 354–68.

von Oech, R. 1983. *A Whack on the Side of the Head*. New York: Warner Brothers Publications.

Ward, A. 1990. Teacher conference. Nanisivik, NWT.

Wiebe, R. 1970. *The Story-Makers*. Toronto: Macmillan of Canada.

York, G. 1990. *The Dispossessed: Life and Death in Native Canada*. London: Vintage U.K.

Index